Yeats and Violence

Yeats
and Violence

MICHAEL WOOD

OXFORD
UNIVERSITY PRESS

OXFORD
UNIVERSITY PRESS

Great Clarendon Street, Oxford, OX2 6DP,
United Kingdom

Oxford University Press is a department of the University of Oxford.
It furthers the University's objective of excellence in research, scholarship,
and education by publishing worldwide. Oxford is a registered trade mark of
Oxford University Press in the UK and in certain other countries

© Michael Wood 2010

The moral rights of the author have been asserted

First published 2010

Published in the United States of America by Oxford University Press
198 Madison Avenue, New York, NY 10016, United States of America

British Library Cataloguing in Publication Data

Data available

ISBN 978-0-19-955766-0

in memory of my grandmother,
Mary Kennedy (1874–1922),
who never went home to Sligo

ACKNOWLEDGEMENTS

All books have many authors but I was particularly lucky in the help I received with this one. It rests on such a mixture of old affection and belatedly acquired knowledge that I really needed all the support I could get, and happily got.

I should like to thank Oxford University Press and the Faculty of English at Oxford for their invitation to give the 2008 Clarendon Lectures, where much of this book began; and especially Andrew McNeillie and Sally Mapstone for their warm welcome.

In Oxford I benefited hugely from the scholarship, kindness, and comments of Christopher Butler, Roy Foster, John Kelly, Hermione Lee, and many others—Roy managed to save me from several serious errors without even seeming to mention them.

I am grateful to the National Humanities Center for awarding me their Frank H. Kenan Fellowship for the spring of 2009. I did much of the later work on this book in the remarkable research atmosphere created and sustained by Geoffrey Harpham and Kent Mullikin and their staff. I should like to thank the Fellows of the Center who shared that time and space with me, and especially Carol Clover, Florence Dore, Rachel Blau-Duplessis, Bob Duplessis, Sarah Farmer, Sandie Welsh, Ruth Yeazell, and the members of the lively Violence and Violation seminar.

I salute and thank the members of my Princeton graduate seminar on Yeats of some years ago, and looking further back still I recall with affection and gratitude the invitation from Jacques Berthoud and Nicole Ward-Jouve to lecture at York, an occasion I took as a first chance to reflect on Yeats' curious courtship of violent events and apparitions. My thanks too to Jonathan Allison for asking me to lecture in New York and to Victor Luftig for the invitation to the University of Virginia.

At Princeton the group I came to think of as the Scansion Club came swiftly and brilliantly to my aid when I was most lost, and I'm happy to write their names out in this non-verse: Jeff Dolven, Meredith Martin, Jim Richardson, Starry Schor, Susan Stewart.

And for conversations short and long, direct and oblique, amateur and expert, all treasured, I thank, along with the members of the above club, Jonathan Allison, Jason Baskin, Alison Booth, Michael Cadden, Holly Chatham, Stefan Collini, Stanley Corngold, Anne Margaret Daniel, Larry Danson, Denis Donoghue, Mark Edmundson, Elizabeth Fowler, Daniel Heller-Roazen, Tal Kastner, Michael Levenson, Victor Luftig, Paul Muldoon, Patrick Parrinder, Zakir Paul, Tom Paulin, James Pethica, John Raimo, Jahan Ramazani, Mark Shiel, Nigel Smith, Chris Turner, Casey Walker, C. K. Williams, Susan Wolfson, Gaby Wood, Patrick Wood, Aron Yaronowicz.

Tony Wood suggested I should look at certain poems by Brecht and Blok, and listened to what I had to say about those poems and much else; what follows would have been much poorer without that look and that listening.

James Longenbach generously took the time to read a whole draft of this book with the strictest of sympathetic eyes, and I am deeply grateful for his subtle response.

And what can I say to Elena except thanks again—and again and again.

M.W.
Princeton, 2009

CONTENTS

Nineteen Hundred and Nineteen   xi

Introduction: Up Close and Serial   1
  1. Violent Men   7
  2. The Platonic Year   48
  3. The Temptation of Form   87
  4. The Old Country   140
  5. Violence upon the Roads   184

Further Reading   229
Index   239

Nineteen Hundred and Nineteen

I

Many ingenious lovely things are gone
That seemed sheer miracle to the multitude,
protected from the circle of the moon
That pitches common things about. There stood
Amid the ornamental bronze and stone
An ancient image made of olive wood—
And gone are Phidias' famous ivories
And all the golden grasshoppers and bees.

We too had many pretty toys when young:
A law indifferent to blame or praise,
To bribe or threat; habits that made old wrong
Melt down, as it were wax in the sun's rays;
Public opinion ripening for so long
We thought it would outlive all future days.
O what fine thought we had because we thought
That the worst rogues and rascals had died out.

All teeth were drawn, all ancient tricks unlearned,
And a great army but a showy thing;
What matter that no cannon had been turned
Into a ploughshare? Parliament and king
Thought that unless a little powder burned
The trumpeters might burst with trumpeting
And yet it lack all glory; and perchance
The guardsmen's drowsy chargers would not prance.

Now days are dragon-ridden, the nightmare
Rides upon sleep: a drunken soldiery
Can leave the mother, murdered at her door,
To crawl in her own blood, and go scot-free;
The night can sweat with terror as before
We pieced our thoughts into philosophy,
And planned to bring the world under a rule,
Who are but weasels fighting in a hole.

He who can read the signs nor sink unmanned
Into the half-deceit of some intoxicant
From shallow wits; who knows no work can stand,
Whether health, wealth or peace of mind were spent
On master-work of intellect or hand,
No honour leave its mighty monument,
Has but one comfort left: all triumph would
But break upon his ghostly solitude.

But is there any comfort to be found?
Man is in love and loves what vanishes,
What more is there to say? That country round
None dared admit, if such a thought were his,
Incendiary or bigot could be found
To burn that stump on the Acropolis,
Or break in bits the famous ivories
Or traffic in the grasshoppers or bees.

II

When Loie Fuller's Chinese dancers enwound
A shining web, a floating ribbon of cloth,
It seemed that a dragon of air
Had fallen among dancers, had whirled them round

Or hurried them off on its own furious path;
So the Platonic Year
Whirls out new right and wrong,
Whirls in the old instead;
All men are dancers and their tread
Goes to the barbarous clangour of a gong.

III

Some moralist or mythological poet
Compares the solitary soul to a swan;
I am satisfied with that,
Satisfied if a troubled mirror show it,
Before that brief gleam of its life be gone,
An image of its state;
The wings half spread for flight,
The breast thrust out in pride
Whether to play, or to ride
Those winds that clamour of approaching night.

A man in his own secret meditation
Is lost amid the labyrinth that he has made
In art or politics;
Some Platonist affirms that in the station
Where we should cast off body and trade
The ancient habit sticks,
And that if our works could
But vanish with our breath
That were a lucky death,
For triumph can but mar our solitude.

The swan has leaped into the desolate heaven:
That image can bring wildness, bring a rage

To end all things, to end
What my laborious life imagined, even
The half-imagined, the half-written page;
O but we dreamed to mend
Whatever mischief seemed
To afflict mankind, but now
That winds of winter blow
Learn that we were crack-pated when we dreamed.

IV

We, who seven years ago
Talked of honour and of truth,
Shriek with pleasure if we show
The weasel's twist, the weasel's tooth.

V

Come let us mock at the great
That had such burdens on the mind
And toiled so hard and late
To leave some monument behind,
Nor thought of the levelling wind.

Come let us mock at the wise;
With all those calendars whereon
They fixed old aching eyes,
They never saw how seasons run,
And now but gape at the sun.

Come let us mock at the good
That fancied goodness might be gay,
And sick of solitude
Might proclaim a holiday:
Wind shrieked—and where are they?

Mock mockers after that
That would not lift a hand maybe
To help good, wise or great
To bar that foul storm out, for we
Traffic in mockery.

VI

Violence upon the roads: violence of horses;
Some few have handsome riders, are garlanded
On delicate sensitive ear or tossing mane,
But wearied running round and round in their courses
All break and vanish, and evil gathers head:
Herodias' daughters have returned again,
A sudden blast of dusty wind and after
Thunder of feet, tumult of images,
Their purpose in the labyrinth of the wind;
And should some crazy hand dare touch a daughter
All turn with amorous cries, or angry cries,
According to the wind, for all are blind.
But now wind drops, dust settles; thereupon
There lurches past, his great eyes without thought
Under the shadow of stupid straw-pale locks,
That insolent fiend Robert Artisson
To whom the love-lorn Lady Kyteler brought
Bronzed peacock feathers, red combs of her cocks.

Introduction:
Up Close and Serial

'This is not an "explication de texte"', Roland Barthes said of his book *S/Z*, although we could be forgiven for thinking it was, and Barthes was anticipating our error. An explication of a novel or story, in his view, follows the plan of a work and distinguishes firmly between frame tale and main narrative, the set-up and the real thing, in order to get at a dominant or central theme. For Barthes there is no such hierarchy. If there is a frame it matters as much as what it notionally contains. 'What accounts for this central equivalence is not the "plan" of *Sarrasine* [the text by Balzac that Barthes is closely studying], but its structure. The structure is not the plan. Therefore, this is not an "explication de texte", *ceci n'est donc pas une explication de texte*.'[1]

The structure is not the plan. The structure supports the text but is not immediately visible;[2] and 'plan' in this context means

[1] Roland Barthes, *S/Z* (Paris: Seuil, 1970), 97; trans. Richard Miller (New York: Hill and Wang, 1974), 90. Translation slightly modified.

[2] Cf. Jacques Derrida, *La dissémination* (Paris: Seuil, 1972), 71. 'Un texte n'est un texte que s'il cache au premier regard, au premier venu, la loi de sa composition et la règle de son jeu'. 'A text is a text only if it conceals from first sight, from the first person to arrive, the law of its composition and the rule of its game'. My translation.

something like narrative layout, the visible surface of the story. The structure of the legend of Oedipus, to follow the famous example given by Claude Lévi-Strauss, concerns the troubled logic of human generation, and plays out in dramatic and dangerous forms the question of whether we are born from the earth or from our parents.[3] Oedipus' name and limp suggest one answer; his excessive relations with mother and father a different one. The plan of the legend tells the story of his killing his father, solving the riddle of the sphinx, marrying his mother, discovering who he is (he is the man who does just these things), blinding himself and sending himself into exile. The structure reflects a continuing cultural preoccupation; the plan represents that preoccupation in a progression of events.

Poems, even longish ones, don't usually have easily identifiable narrative plans; but they do have sequences of thematic and tonal movements that we can think of as the equivalent of plans, and they certainly have structures. The plan of W. B. Yeats' 'Nineteen Hundred and Nineteen', the poem that is the subject of this book, might crudely be paraphrased in the terms I offer below. Yeats called the whole thing a poem, and he called its six numbered parts poems too—so there is already an interesting question about the dependence of the divisions on the whole and vice-versa, and about degrees of independence. This question is deepened by the formal variety of the poems/ parts. (I've called these elements 'parts' throughout, as 'section' seems divisive, and 'poem' a little confusing.)

---

[3] Claude Lévi-Strauss 'La structure du mythe', in *Anthropologie structurale* (Paris: Plon, 1955), 227–55.

I

Many ingenious lovely things are gone, like the art objects of ancient Greece. We had some lovely things too, or thought we had, like law and civilized behaviour. We had forgotten that lovely things go and others stay, or always return; like war and crime. We live in violent times now, all our ideas of rule overturned or destroyed. We thought we were philosophers, but we were/are only weasels. Surely we've always known that nothing lasts, and that worldly achievement is merely an interruption of the splendid solitude of the mind. Is this any comfort, if we always love vanishing things? Even in Greece, no one would admit to the thought that anyone could burn or break or sell those lovely objects.

II

The cloths waved by Loie Fuller and her dancers seemed to be a dragon that was in turn waving them, hurrying them off in the direction it chose. The Platonic Year is like this dragon, whirling out new right and wrong, and whirling old right and wrong back in again. We are Loie Fuller's dancers, and behind the apparent dragon, the effect created by our waving cloths, is the barbarous beat we cannot refuse—the beat of long-term fate, it seems, rather than history or any individual destiny.

III

The soul is like a swan ready to take flight. To take flight out of its bodily life, the place of art, politics, the labyrinth of the world that is too much with us. But the thought of the swan having flown makes us rage against the world we are supposed to be happy to leave, and happy to have done nothing in, at least according to the Platonist. After all, what we were doing in the labyrinth was trying to make things better. An illusion; worse, a crazy notion.

IV

Seven years ago we were honourable men. Now we are weasels, and delighted to be weasels.

V

So let us mock those honourable men, the great, wise, and good, for their folly. And then mock ourselves, because mockery is no better than what it mocks—and maybe worse, because we're still in business.

VI

Violence is on the move. There are mysterious horses on the road; the ancient gods can be seen in the wind. And when the wind drops, we see the mindless hero of an old magical history lurching past, the obscure object of a none too obscure desire.

The structure of the poem rests on the difficult relations between art and fragility, law and violence, solitude and action, mockery and whatever alternative there may be to it, revelation and disenchantment. But since 'Nineteen Hundred and Nineteen' is a poem and not an exercise in binary logic, all of these apparent oppositions or distinctions are disturbed and unstable. Art is fragile; law itself may be violent; solitude may have no recourse but to leave litter in the world of action; there may be no alternative to mockery. Revelation may *be* disenchantment, and the whole poem in one sense is about what happens when we can't tell the difference between a march and a lurch. The structure, in other words, can't do without the plan. But the plan without the structure may tend to look as if it's drifting or pursuing chance associations.

This book is an *explication de texte* that is also interested in structure. It seeks to give an account of the way the above elements (and a few more) meet and clash in the poem, of the tunes they make, and of the ways in which the whole formation connects to the historical world. My readings are consecutive and distributed across the whole book. Chapters 1 and 2 consider the first three parts of the poem; Chapter 3 looks at the formal properties of the work as a whole; Chapters 4 and 5 concentrate on the last three parts. I could say these commentaries are staggered across the book, but then the pun in the verb becomes almost luridly relevant and insistent. I am thinking of the *OED*'s 'To bewilder, perplex, nonplus; to render helpless by a shock of amazement (or occasionally horror). In passive, to be perplexed or astonished at'. As distinct from the same source's 'To arrange (an event or action) so that its implementation is spread over a period of time'.

Henry James defines criticism as the action of the mind 'reaching out for the reasons of its interest', which is in turn 'the very education of our imaginative life'.[4] I think we may also need to reach out for the reasons of our pleasure and distress and bafflement, and perhaps also reach out for more than reasons. A friend kindly asked me, in some surprise, why I would want to write in detail about this poem—when there are so many other, less desolate ones I could have chosen, was his implication. It's a good question, and I hope this book provides some sort of answer. But I should like to say at the outset that we can be strongly drawn, and need to understand why we are so strongly drawn, not to what disturbs us but to memorable formulations of what disturbs us, words and phrases and images that allow

[4] Henry James, 'The New Novel', in *Literary Criticism* (New York: Library of America, 1984), 24.

us to keep remembering what we would rather forget. There are uncomfortable old companions who never lose their capacity to bother us, and we may be grateful to them for that.

I want to say of 'Nineteen Hundred and Nineteen' what Frank Kermode very well said of 'In Memory of Major Robert Gregory': 'It is a poem worthy of much painful reading.'[5] Worthy of much pleasurable reading too, of course; but the pleasure is not a denial of the pain. This book is at heart a response not only to the work of W. B. Yeats, and not only to a particular poem by W. B. Yeats but to particular lines within that poem, lines that have never left my mind since I first read them, and that seemed to be asking me to do something about them that I was too lazy or troubled or dazzled to do. They come from the first and last parts of the work:

> Now days are dragon-ridden; the nightmare
> Rides upon sleep: a drunken soldiery
> Can leave the mother, murdered at her door,
> To crawl in her own blood, and go scot-free …
>
> But now wind drops, dust settles; and thereupon
> There lurches past, his great eyes without thought
> Under the shadow of stupid, straw-pale locks,
> That insolent fiend Robert Artisson
> To whom the lovelorn Lady Kyteler brought
> Bronzed peacock feathers, red combs of her cocks.

The recurrence of the word 'now' has a great deal to do with the power of these lines. What's interesting about *now* is how it shifts in time; and how it is never without a *then*.

---

[5] Frank Kermode, *Romantic Image* (New York: Vintage, 1964), 30.

1

Violent Men

'Then ... now ... what difficulties here, for the mind'

SAMUEL BECKETT, *Happy Days*

'Bearings taken, markings, cardinal points,
Options, obstinacies, dug heels, and distance,
Here and there and now and then, a stance'

SEAMUS HEANEY, *District and Circle*

I

Yeats is a poet almost everyone associates with violence. We think of 'Leda and the Swan', of the bombs and broken civilizations of 'Lapis Lazuli', of all the deaths and executions in the plays. Roy Foster writes of the poet's 'old theme of the gestation of violence',[1] and Helen Vendler reminds us of the recurrence of 'the enigma of human violence' in the work.[2] Ezra Pound said

---

[1] Roy Foster, *W. B. Yeats: A Life II. The Arch-Poet* (Oxford: Oxford University Press, 2003), 24.

[2] Helen Vendler, *Our Secret Discipline: Yeats and Lyric Form* (Cambridge: Harvard University Press, 2007), 64.

Yeats understood 'violent emotion' better than anyone else.[3] When an Indian visitor asked the poet in 1937 if he had a message for the sub-continent Yeats grasped a Japanese sword—perhaps he was thinking of the Greater Asia—and said, 'Conflict. More conflict.'[4] And in a late poem he wrote that

> Even the wisest man grows tense
> With some sort of violence
> Before he can accomplish fate
> Know his work or choose his mate.[5]

And yet Yeats very rarely uses the word violence itself in his verse: four mentions in the whole of the *Collected Poems*, two of them in one line of 'Nineteen Hundred and Nineteen'. The other two are in 'Meditations in Time of Civil War' and in the lines I have just quoted from 'Under Ben Bulben'. There are only six uses of the adjective 'violent'—again two of them in a single poem. How can this be? Perhaps Yeats doesn't name violence much because for him it is everywhere. Or shall we say he doesn't name it more often because for him it is not usually a concept but a practice that has many names and shapes and above all many instances, and it is the instances that matter?

Violence changes for Yeats, and his own relation to it changes. There is something both foggy and cosy about the phrase 'some

---

[3] James Longenbach, *Stone Cottage: Pound, Yeats and Modernism* (Oxford: Oxford University Press, 1988), 185.

[4] W. J. McCormack, *Blood Kindred: W. B. Yeats, the Life the Death, the Politics* (London: Pimlico, 2005), 25, citing Richard Ellman.

[5] W. B. Yeats, *The Variorum Edition of the Poems*, ed. Peter Allt and Russell K. Alspach (New York: Macmillan, 1957), 638.

sort of violence'; and we may feel the same about Yeats' late enthusiasm for conflict, which had all kinds of connections to his interest in fascism. When he says, in a late pamphlet, that 'if human violence is not embodied in our institutions, the young will not give them their affection, nor the young and old their loyalty',[6] we may not like the sort of institutions he is contemplating, and we may suspect that he is merely gesturing towards a truth that he once understood better and feared more: that there are roads, inside and outside the mind, that cannot be unblocked by peaceful means. This is precisely what Denis Donoghue points to when he reminds us of Yeats' interest in 'violent annunciation'. 'We recognize', Donoghue finely says, 'the clenched paradigm of Yeats' later poetry.'[7] My interest is in how clenched, and how notionally unclenchable, the paradigm is; and in how early it asserts its rule.

II

I'm going to begin at some distance from 'Nineteen Hundred and Nineteen' but still inside the work of Yeats, with a poem that I believe constitutes Yeats as an authority on violence, and that

[6] W. B. Yeats, *On the Boiler*, cited in Frank Kermode, 'The Anglo-Irish Hyphen', *The Hopkins Review*, NS 1.1 (Winter 2008), 114.

[7] Denis Donoghue, *Adam's Curse: Reflections on Religion and Literature* (Notre Dame: University of Notre Dame Press, 2001), 5. The context of Yeats' remark is a note on 'Leda and the Swan', where he says 'the editor of a political review' had asked him for a poem, prompting in him thoughts of the excesses of individualism and demagoguery he associates with Hobbes and the French Revolution. 'Then I thought, "Nothing is now possible but some movement from above preceded by some violent annunciation"'. *Variorum Edition*, 828.

also, I hope, will allow us to make a start on the question of what a poem, as distinct from any other sort of proposition or utterance, may have to tell us, or show us, about violence or anything else. The poem is 'The Magi', first published in the magazine *Poetry* and in *The New Statesman* in May 1914, and collected in the volume *Responsibilities* the same year. The poem doesn't contain the word 'violence' but it starts with the word 'now'.

> Now as at all times I can see in the mind's eye,
> In their stiff, painted clothes, the pale unsatisfied ones
> Appear and disappear in the blue depth of the sky
> With all their ancient faces like rain-beaten stones,
> And all their helms of silver hovering side by side,
> And all their eyes still fixed, hoping to find once more,
> Being by Calvary's turbulence unsatisfied,
> The uncontrollable mystery on the bestial floor.[8]

These are the Magi of the New Testament, the Three Kings of every school nativity play. They have called on Herod, delivered their gifts to the Christ child and deciding not to let Herod know what they have seen, they have 'departed into their own country another way' (Matthew 2: 12). They may have had a 'cold coming of it', as T. S. Eliot and Lancelot Andrewes thought, but they seem to be entirely benevolent figures. Yet here they are again, Yeats' poem suggests, 'unsatisfied', eager for turbulence. Perhaps they have always been here, 'now as at all times', waiting for the right human mind to accommodate them. The repetition of 'unsatisfied' is very troubling because we don't associate these

---

[8] *Variorum Edition*, 318.

figures with any appetite at all, even benign. But they came to Bethlehem, it now seems, not for what they saw there but for what they knew about or hoped for from a later scene in the same life, although outside the walls of Jerusalem this time: 'Calvary's turbulence'. The phrase refers no doubt to the whole grisly drama of the crucifixion of Christ and the two thieves, but it may also have, probably does have, a more specific referent: the shaking of the earth and darkness of the sky at the moment of Christ's death: 'And, behold, the veil of the temple was rent in twain from the top to the bottom; and the earth did quake, and the rocks rent' (Matthew 27: 52). Turbulence indeed. This, it seems, is what the Magi were after when they sought the child in the manger, and it is what they are after now as they await, 'all their eyes still fixed', the second coming of ... what? A disturbance, or the early incarnation of a coming disturbance, even more earth-shaking than Christianity has been for the last two thousand years? 'Once more' is extraordinarily eerie. Last time they saw the helpless child as an 'uncontrollable mystery' and the peaceable animals in the stable as a sort of heraldic emblem of bestiality. If they could do this to centuries of Christian iconography before it even got started, and also think the crucifixion was not turbulent enough, what can they be looking for now?

In one sense, the answer is easy. These are creatures from a mythology Yeats developed over the years, a view of history as moving in 2,000-year cycles, of which more in another chapter. The Magi know this view intimately, the Christian cycle of which they were such famous witnesses is about to end, and they are ready to attest the transition to the next. As Jeffares puts it, 'The Magi are unsatisfied ... because they represent Yeats' belief that the Christian revelation was not final ... Christ is uncontrollable because he is not final.'[9]

But there would be all kinds of ways of representing cyclical history without having the appetite for violence that becomes the dominant mood of this poem. The Magi are not looking for change, which may perhaps be turbulent, as historical changes often are. They are looking for turbulence. Why would they want this, hope to find it? Perhaps because they are figures for, among other things, our own hostility to, our alienation from the very life we live, as Yeats himself suggested: 'I had noticed once again', he said in relation to this poem, 'how all thought among us is frozen into "something other than human life".'[10] He takes the phrase 'something other than human life' from Blake, who was referring to the Houses of Parliament: 'they seem to me to be something else besides human life'. But Yeats is also quoting himself. He told his journal that women 'give all to an opinion as if it were some terrible stone doll'. 'They grow cruel', he said, 'and all this is done for "something other than human life".'[11] We can think of the hearts 'enchanted to a stone' of 'Easter 1916'. The Magi are our frozen thoughts, our cold and continuing appetite for the disruption of human appetite.

We can go further, I think. The Magi are unsatisfied by Calvary's turbulence not because it was insufficient or not final but because they cannot be satisfied. They are by definition the pale, unsatisfied ones, something like Yeats' personal version of

---

[9] A. N. Jeffares, *A New Commentary on the Poems of W. B. Yeats* (Stanford: Stanford University Press, 1984), 126.

[10] *Variorum Edition*, 820.

[11] W. B. Yeats, *Autobiographies* (New York: Scribner, 1999), 372.

the Greek Furies. They are insatiety itself, and what they long to see on the bestial floor is not what the uncontrollable mystery means or foreshadows, but the very shape of the uncontrollable, attractive to them in the measure that each case will be more uncontrollable than the last. Is such a desire intelligible? Not entirely, I think. But it is perceptible, and we feel it, I think, in the strange, horrified curiosity which is the main mood this poem inspires in us—inspires in me at any rate. The concentration and patience of the Magi are infectious and inordinately compelling. The last thing I really want to see in human history is another uncontrollable mystery on the bestial floor; but part of me, at least when I'm reading this poem, wants to see it all the same, is anxious to share the Magi's vision when it comes, so I too am 'hoping to find' something in the turbulence. I know, as the Magi would also if they lived anywhere other than in Yeats' mythology, that the vision is not going to come, that there is only the passion of the endless waiting, the apocalypse always postponed, but that doesn't diminish the passion, or the suspense.

The suspense concerns not the experience of violence but the witnessing of it. The Magi are not going to participate in whatever act of succession they find to Calvary's turbulence, and it seems likely that, to whatever degree we share their sinister interest, we too are waiting for, let's say, news—news which can only be violent because we have got ourselves into a historical condition where only violence is news. This was neither more nor less true in 1914 than it is now. To be really precise, though, the Magi are not waiting for the news. They know the news. They are waiting for the violent performance of the news.

The word that is hovering here is 'revelation', and it is of course the word Yeats uses in 'The Second Coming': 'Surely some revelation is at hand'. At hand: not occurring, not occurred, and not in any remote future. This is one of two key moments in so many of Yeats' poems: just before. The other moment is not exactly symmetrical, since it is not 'just after' but long enough after for hindsight to claim that the intervening event has wrecked the whole earlier world. 'Nineteen Hundred and Nineteen' is poised between these two times, in reverse order: first the aftermath of the wrecking event, then the waiting for immediate ugly revelation.

III

Graham Hough once said that like any sane person he was afraid of violence. I was struck by the phrase because I thought it was bold of him to say it. At that time, around 1968, many of us thought, or thought we thought, that some forms of violence were necessary, and only the fearful bourgeoisie condemned all violence—and even they were pretending, because they didn't condemn violence when it was on their side. But the phrase was not just bold, it seemed deeply, necessarily true, in a way I didn't understand at the time. That was why it haunted me. Graham Hough certainly knew what he was talking about, having been a prisoner of war in a Japanese camp—a series of camps, no doubt, since he was interned in Malaya and Siam from 1942 to 1945. And he wasn't comfortably condemning violence, just confessing his fear of it. A fear of violence wouldn't save you from violence, it might even throw you into it. It wouldn't even save you from committing violence, in a rage or for some thought-out moral or political cause. But the fear would remain, whatever else went away. That fear would be your sanity. If you were not afraid of violence, either you were not sane or you were not really talking about violence at all.

In 'Nineteen Hundred and Nineteen' and other poems of that period (1919–1922) Yeats both dramatizes frightful violence and suggests that violence may alter the world. It could wreck ideals certainly, but just as possibly might open the door to a new order. The wreckage was real for him, and the apocalypse was always just around the corner. Or when it came it turned out not to be the apocalypse. However, he continued, at least through the 1920s, to understand that the promise of violence was inseparable from everything that made you afraid of it. Violence in this sense might have something of the status of the sacred as Agamben defines it in *Homo Sacer*. The sacred, Agamben proposes, is not either holy or monstrous, or both holy and monstrous, or ambivalently poised between the two, as anthropologists have thought.[12] It is what lies at the basis of the very distinction between holiness and monstrosity. Violence, similarly, might be what separates, in the act, what we hoped from what we feared.

We can't ignore or wish to ignore the generalized presence of violence in the world, what David Lloyd calls 'the ubiquitous and seemingly endless violence that is constitutive of modernity',[13]

---

[12] Giorgio Agamben, *Homo Sacer*, trans. Daniel Heller-Roazen (Stanford: Stanford University Press, 1998), 82–3. Agamben says something similar about the law: 'the juridical order does not originally present itself simply as sanctioning a transgressive fact but instead constitutes itself through the repetition of the same act without any sanction, that is, as an exceptional case' (*Homo Sacer*, 26).

[13] David Lloyd, *Irish Times* (Dublin: Field Day, 2008), 29.

and not only of modernity, of course. We need to recognize the symbolic and systemic violence Slavoj Zizek emphatically points to as well as the violence he calls subjective, 'violence performed by a clearly identifiable agent'.[14] Walter Benjamin writes of 'legal violence', *Rechtsgewalt,* meaning the violence of the law itself,[15] and even Hannah Arendt speaks of 'state-owned means of violence'.[16]

Still, there is a problem with the equation of violence and force effected by the German word 'Gewalt', which means both things, and the problem trails into much political theory.[17] I don't believe violence always can or needs to be separated from force, even where the language allows it, since both the strict separation of the two terms and their collapse into a single concept can be useful and both moves can be tendentious. The equation of force and violence, for example, tends to inculpate authorities; a strong distinction between the two tends to put the blame on rogue individuals or agencies. But even this description evokes only a very broad rule

[14] Slavoj Zizek, *Violence* (London: Profile Books, 2008), 1.

[15] Walter Benjamin, 'Critique of Violence'. In *Selected* Writings vol. 1, ed. Marcus Bullock and Michael W. Jennings (Cambridge, Mass.: Harvard University Press, 1996), 238.

[16] Hannah Arendt, *On Violence* (New York: Harcourt Brace, 1970), 48.

[17] In a public letter to Einstein Freud suggested replacing the word *Macht,* 'might' (in the phrase 'the relationship of right and might') with 'the shriller, harder word *Gewalt*', in this case closer in meaning to violence than to force. In *Warum Krieg? (Why War?)* (Dijon: Internationales Institut für Geistige Zusammenarbeit, 1937), 27. My translation.

of thumb,[18] and I don't think we can settle the matter by handy definitions, as Arendt nobly tries to do.[19] Language and usage have their own life, and will close and open gaps in all kinds of different ways.

However, the fact that words are slippery doesn't mean they don't have meanings. Raymond Williams' difficulties with the word 'violence' are exemplary in this respect, and I'm certainly not going to do better than he could.[20] Let me suggest though that all the easier uses of the word 'violence', whatever place they come from on the political spectrum, and including Yeats' own pronouncements later in his life, lose a great deal by blurring or softening the edginess the word may contain, and we shall very often need a way of distinguishing between the presence of troops, for example, and the behaviour of those same troops on a particular day or in a particular mood. In bad times, we need a way of distinguishing not only between a police force and police brutality but between measures backed by force and

[18] Cf. Arno Mayer, *The Furies* (Princeton: Princeton University Press, 2000), 74. 'Both conceptually and in practice, force and violence are construed as opposites, though the boundaries between them are forever being tested, contested, and adjusted.' This is true when they are not being construed as identical, conceptually and in practice.

[19] '*Power* corresponds to the human ability not just to act but to act in concert ... *Strength* unequivocally designates something in the singular, an individual entity ... *Force* ... should be reserved ... for the 'force of nature' or the 'force of circumstances' ... *Authority* ... can be vested in persons ... or it can be vested in offices ... *Violence* ... is distinguished by its instrumental character' (*On Violence*, 44–5).

[20] Raymond Williams, *Keywords* (London: Fontana, 1976), 329–31.

measures implemented through violence. Whatever else it is, violence isn't bland—or 'polite', as Roland Barthes says.[21]

My Yeats-inspired resistance to the concept of legal or systemic violence doesn't have to do with the validity of the idea but with the level of generality at which it operates. Here I want to borrow a theory of explanation from Philip Pettit because it helps me to pause over the word 'random', which is the tempting label for the kind of violence I am interested in.[22] It isn't random if we shift our level of explanation. But it *feels* random, and that feeling matters even if random is finally the wrong word because some sort of causality is in play. I can't explain, for example, why a particular person is mugged at a particular time in downtown Trenton or downtown almost anywhere in the UK these days, but I can make a plausible show of explaining why downtown Trenton or downtown Lincoln is a good spot for muggings and why so many muggings occur there: empty streets, unemployment, poor policing, drink, drugs etc. The particular case, in other words, should and perhaps must always cause surprise, will entirely refuse explanation unless we move our game up a

[21] 'There is the violence residing in all constraint of the individual by the group. This is why one may say there is a violence of the law, of laws, of the police, the state … But it's a diffuse violence, dry, polite' (Roland Barthes, *The Grain of the Voice*, trans. Linda Coverdale (London: Jonathan Cape, 1985), 308).

[22] Philip Pettit and Frank Jackson, 'Structural Explanation and Social Theory', in *Reduction, Explanation and Realism*, ed David Charles and Kathleen Lennon (Oxford: Oxford University Press, 1992); and Philip Pettit and Frank Jackson, 'In Defence of Explanatory Ecumenism', *Economics and Philosophy*, vol 8, 1992.

notch. The more general account shouldn't surprise us at all—it should make the very sense that surprise must deny. But we can't just swap or abandon one level for another without loss. Poetry, I want to suggest, refuses to move away from the surprise, from the effect of the random, and I'd like to think Wallace Stevens means something like this when he says 'the disorder of poetry is its history'.[23] It refuses order for the sake of history, as we may refuse, temporarily, the smoother reaches of theory for the sake of the lessons of surprise.

Zizek seems to suggest this approach when he says 'there is something inherently mystifying in a direct confrontation' with violence[24]—a direct verbal confrontation, he means and one that, precisely, seeks to demystify. And in the sharpest essay I know on this question, David Lloyd distinguishes between violence and rage—even Benjamin didn't talk of legal rage. Lloyd says that rage

stands *before* the law- and subject-making moment of violence ... It neither institutes nor destroys: it is resolutely non-narrative and gives rise to nothing out of its stasis, and though, indeed, it may give way almost immediately to violence, it remains another moment with another logic. It is sheer manifestation, but of nothing.[25]

What I want to suggest—or rather what my reading of Yeats suggests to me—is that there is a moment within vio-

---

[23] Wallace Stevens, *Letters* (New York: Knopf, 1966), 47.

[24] *Violence*, 3.

[25] David Lloyd, 'Rage against the Divine', *South Atlantic Quarterly*, 106:2 (Spring 2007), 353–4.

lence that is also non-narrative and seemingly prior to the law and the human subject. It is not necessarily a moment of rage, although it could be. It is always a moment of turbulence, to return to what the Magi were after. Violence as Yeats helps us to understand it—whether personal, political, or apocalyptic—is always sudden and surprising, visible, unmistakable, inflicts or promises injury and is fundamentally uncontrollable.

IV

'Now days are dragon-ridden ...' The 'now' that lies behind these lines, commentators tell us, is very specific: a certain day in November 1920. The place was Kiltartan, in Galway, and a group of Auxiliaries, shooting from a truck as they drove past, killed a woman holding a baby in her arms. Yeats wasn't there—he was in Oxford—but Lady Gregory told him about it and told her Journal about it too.

Nov 5. A. writes, 'The milk girl says a young woman was shot yesterday at Kiltartan by a lorry of passing military ...' Then Ellen told me it was Malachi Quinn's young wife who had been shot dead—with her child in her arms ... Foley says it is dangerous now to be on the road, and it was dangerous to stay in the house at night ...

Malachi was in Gort when it happened, they sent for him ... There were 89 cars at the funeral. 'Burning would be too good for the Black-and-Tans,' J. says. Tim says they have been firing continuously as they pass, his sick daughter cannot sleep ... They say now it was not done by them, but the dying woman herself was the witness, told her mother and the priest that she had been shot by the Black-and-Tans ...

MAGYAR INVASIONS

ARAB INVASIONS

VIKING INVASIONS

Norman Conquest
of southern Italy
and Sicily
1061-91

Silk industry started
in Sicily
1150

GROWTH OF FEUDALISM

Norman Conquest
of England
1066

Moslem conquest of Spain
11-715

Use of watermill
(about 850)

Kettle drums
and trumpets introduced
to Europe

Moslems defeated
in Spain
1139

Charlemagne crowned
Holy Roman Emperor
800

Re-introduction of gold coins

Stirrups introduced
to Europe

Horseshoes come
into common usage

Vikings sack Lindisfarne
793

First windmills 1190

Sugar planted
in Egypt

Earliest Hebrew manuscript
of Old Testament
895

Moslems overrun Anatolia
1071

Second Crusade
1147-49

ABBASIDS 750-1100

Third Crusade
1189-92

Moslem conquest
f North Africa
00-710

Paper manufactured
in Egypt 900

First Crusade 1096-99

Saladin captures Jerusalem 1187

ANG DYNASTY 618-907

Paper money
in China

SUNG DYNASTY 960-1279

opulation explosion
China

THE FIVE DYNASTIES
907-969

Glossary

Alliance: a political agreement between two or more countries or tribes.
Auxiliary: soldier recruited to the Roman army from a non-Roman tribe.
Barbarian: the Roman term for any member of a foreign tribe.
Bastion: literally, part of a fortification but it is also used to mean a defence or stronghold.
Cohort: a body of about 500 Roman soldiers.
Confederation or federation: a political union between several tribes or states.
Crusade: a military expedition undertaken by Christians to recapture the Holy Land from the Moslems. There were eight crusades in the Middle Ages.
Duchy: territory ruled by a duke or duchess.
Feud: hatred and hostility between two people, tribes or even countries.
Foray: to make a raid in search of booty.
Garrison: soldiers living in a town or country location in order to protect it.
Guardian: someone who protects and manages the affairs of a child until he is old enough to think and act for himself.
Heretic: someone who holds opinions which go against the teachings of the established Church.
Legionary: a foot soldier in the Roman army. Legionaries were recruited from Roman citizens.
Mace: a heavy club, often with spikes on it. It is sometimes used today as a ceremonial symbol of authority or sovereignty.
Mercenary: a soldier who fights for money rather than loyalty to a country or cause.
Pagan: a member of a tribe that did not believe in the Christian God.
Palisade: a fence of wooden stakes.
Sack: to plunder a conquered city.
Standard: a flag or carved figure raised on a pole to indicate the rallying point of a legion. Soldiers felt great loyalty to their own standard.
Steppes: vast, treeless plains, especially in central Asia.
Treaty: a peace agreement between countries or states.
Veteran: a soldier who has had long military service, or a retired soldier.

Index

Bold face indicates pages on which illustrations appear.

Aachen 33
Acquitaine 19
Adrianople, Battle of (378) 16
Aethelbert, King of Kent 57
Aethelread the Unready 36
Africa, North 8, 11, 21, 36, 38, 40, 42, 44
Aëtius 20, 22, 23
Agiluf's Cross **31**
Alamanni 17, 26
Alans 16, 18, 19
Alaric 18-19, **56**
Alexius, Emperor 50
Alfred the Great 35, 36
Allah 42 *see also* Islam
Almohades 44
Almoravids 44
Alp Arslan 40
Altai Mountains 22
America 36, 37
Ambrosius 24
Anatolia 40
Angles 24
Anglo-Saxons *see* Saxons
Antioch 40, 50
Arabs 6, 30, 40, 42, 44, 50
Aragon 44
Arcadius 18
Arianism 26
Armenia 40
Arnulfings 30
Arthur, King 24
Asding Vandals 17
Athelstan, King of Wessex 36
Attila 22-3
Augustine, St 39, **57**
Auxiliary troops (Roman) **11**
Austrasia 30
Avars 38

Bavaria 38
Belgrade 57
Belisarius 26, 40
Berbers 44
Black Sea 23
Bleda 22-3
Bohemond d' Hauteville 50
Book of Durrow **25**
Britain 12-13, 18, 24-5
Brittany 38
Bulgars 40
Burgundians 17, 20, 26
Burgundy 38
Byzantine Church 32
Byzantium (Eastern Empire) 15, 18, 23, 26-7, 40-1, 42-3, 47, 50, 56, 57

Carloman 31-3
Carolingians 32-3, 34, 35, 38
    art **33**
Castile 44
Catapults **12-13**
Cavalry
    Byzantine 40, 41

Frankish 32-3
    Roman 14-15
Celts 24-5
Centuries 13
Charlemagne 31-3, 38, 39
Charles, King of Franks 46
Charles Martel 30-1, 33, 42
Chartres 46
Childeric I, King of Franks 56
China 9, 16, 22, 42
Chlodovic *see* Clovis
Christianity 15, 26, 27, 30, 32, 39, 50, 54, 56, 57
Clovis 26, **56**
Cohorts 11, 12-3
Cnut (Canute) 37
Constantine the Great 15, 56, 57
Constantine (general) 18, 24
Constantine Calorus 56
Constantinople 15, 23, 26, 40, 42, 53, 56, 57
Cordoba 44
Cornwall 25
Crusades 50-3
Crusading States 52-3

Danelaw 36
Danes 34, 35, 36, 39, 48 *see also* Vikings
Danube, River 15-16, 23, 32, 40
Dark Ages 28
Dorylaeum, Battle of (1097) 50

East Anglia (Kingdom) 24, 25, 36
Edward the Confessor 37, 48
Edward, King of Wessex 36
Egypt 8, 42, 53
Elbe, River 32
Emirates, Spanish 44
England 25, 36-7, 48-9, 57
Eric Bloodaxe, King of Northumberland 36
Essex (Kingdom) 25
Ethelbert *see* Aethelbert
Ethelread *see* Aethelread

Fealty 46
Feudal system 31, 33, 54, 55
France 19, 26, 29, 37, 38, 42, 56
Franks 6, 17, 20, 26, 28, 29-33, 35, 38, 42, 46, 50-3, 56
Frisians 30, 35
Fyrd 49

Galseric 21
Gaul 18, 20, 23, 57
Germanic peoples 17, 21, 26-7, 57
Germany 18, 38, 56
Gibraltar, Straits of 21, 44
Godfrey of Bouillon 50
Goths 16, 18-21, 26-7, 28, 30
Granada, Kingdom of 44
Greek Fire 42, **43**
Greenland 36, 37
Gregory I, Pope 57
Guiscard, Robert 47
Guthrum (Viking leader) 36
Guy of Lusignan 53

Nov 9. Malachi Quinn came to see me looking dreadfully worn and changed and his nerves broken, he could hardly speak when he came in … He believes they shot her on purpose—they came so close…

Nov 18. I was so angry at the official report of Eileen Quinn's shooting—beginning 'the enquiry was open to all but few chose to attend it'[26]

The enquiry, it seems, was open only to witnesses, and soon over. It was suggested the men were just firing into the air, so that a bullet 'might have come down perpendicularly and struck' the young woman. Lady Gregory is told that 'an officer with a dark countenance and a Scotch accent took it all into his hands' and that the President of the Court, nominally conducting the enquiry, 'seemed afraid' of this officer.[27] A grim and no doubt unintentional pun lies in Yeats' phrase in the poem about the drunken soldiery going 'scot-free'. Of course the scot in 'scot-free' has no connection with Scotland, but the sound is there, and the unconscious is no great respecter of etymologies.

There are myths and passions lurking everywhere in these sentences: the officer's dark countenance, Malachi Quinn's theory about the men's intentions, the angry phrase about burning the Black-and-Tans. We need to remember that with this last Journal entry we are only three days away from (the first) Bloody Sunday, when IRA units killed a dozen suspected intelligence officers in Dublin, and Auxiliaries killed eleven civilians

[26] Lady Gregory, *Journals*, vol 1 (New York: Oxford University Press, 1978), 197, 199, 201.

[27] Ibid. 202.

at a Gaelic football match. And of course the British military authority was not the only agency cooking up fantastic stories about its acts of violence, along the lines of an innocent bullet falling perpendicularly and killing a person by accident.

In May of the following year, in the same region, Margaret Gregory, Robert Gregory's widow, was the only survivor of an IRA ambush, and the following unlikely tale was concocted. The other woman in the car under attack, being 'a deadly shot with a revolver, picked up her husband's weapon and pinned down the attackers ... Having no option, the ambushers killed the woman'.[28] This is a much later Nationalist account. Fergus Campbell, my source for this story, calls it 'implausible' and says 'it is more likely that Mrs Blake was deliberately shot in revenge for the killing of Mrs Ellen Quinn (who was also pregnant) at nearby Kiltartan by the RIC the previous November'.[29] I'm not sure how visibly pregnant Mrs Blake was, and it seems unlikely that the soldiers would have spotted Mrs Quinn's pregnancy from their truck—and the child in her arms ought to have given her a modicum of protection anyway. But the actual death of two pregnant women is certainly part of the atmosphere of violence as a disorder of history, and Campbell even speaks of 'generally accepted rules of combat' that did not permit 'killing a pregnant woman'.[30] I don't know of a rule of combat that permits killing innocent bystanders at all, and the idea that Mrs Blake might have been murdered legitimately if it were not for her condition is truly bizarre.

[28] Fergus Campbell, *Land and Revolution: Nationalist Politics in the West of Ireland 1891–1921* (Oxford: Oxford University Press, 2005), 277.

[29] Ibid. 277–8.   [30] Ibid. 277.

But it is bizarre in an understandable and revealing way. We are in a world without rules but where it still feels as if rules are being broken—if not the rules we used to have, then the ones we believe we ought to have. We are caught between immediate, random-feeling violence and the half-explanation that is the next stage up towards generality. The word 'revenge' is a symptom of this in-between state, and there was a more current contemporary word: reprisal. The Bishop of Ardagh, in a letter to a local MP, called Lloyd George's government 'the Reprisal Government', and insisted, although he said firmly that he was 'no Sinn Feiner', that the acts of violence against civilians being committed all around him were 'connived at if not originated by the Government'.[31] Lily Yeats, the poet's sister, also said she was 'no Sinn Feiner', or least she wasn't in 1919, 'just a mild nationalist, but now ...'.[32] The cause of this change was a set of atrocities

[31] Letter to Joseph Devlin, 5 Nov. 1920. House of Commons Archive. A milder but subtly expressed view is that of Robert Kee, *The Green Flag, Volume Three: Ourselves Alone* (London: Quartet Books, 1976), 110: 'the government seems to have awoken slowly to the political consequences of reprisals, concentrating at first on the wholly irrelevant point that while deplorable they were understandable. They did not seem understandable to the innocent people who usually suffered from them.' Elsewhere in the same volume [p.93] Kee reminds us that Black and Tan atrocities, which have often been depicted as part of the long, ongoing offensive of the English against the Irish, didn't get under way until early 1920—before that Michael Collins and his men were doing pretty much all the apparently random killing. But then the first Black and Tan rampage was repeated so often and so soon that 'it would seem as if there had never been a time when such things did not happen'.

[32] *The Arch-Poet*, 181.

by the Black and Tans and a truck driving by with 'Reprisals Galore' written on its side. Reprisals, notionally, were random killings after a policeman or a soldier had been murdered. The very term, in other words, combines causality and chance. There is a reason why this is happening, but no reason why it is happening to you. This is precisely how terrorism works, of course, whether it is activated by the state or against the state. Accidents are part of the fear-inspiring plan; the unruly, excessive actions of soldiers or gunmen are both unpredictable and calculated. Reprisals offer, in the language of David Lloyd's essay on rage, a narrative that doesn't know its own limits or procedures, and so isn't entirely a narrative; a logic that seems broken even before it starts to operate. Reprisals are the reason for violence, but no one knows what forms of violence reprisals permit and disallow. The fantastic stories I've evoked, the bullet falling out of the sky, the victim who turns out to be a crack shot, themselves demonstrate, however feebly, that no one, on either side, thinks everything is permitted.

Yeats' poem 'Reprisals', a sort of trial run for a part of 'Nineteen Hundred and Nineteen' and a work he didn't publish in his lifetime, arises from this context. He wrote it in November 1920, soon after the killing of Mrs Quinn and Bloody Sunday—he didn't compose 'Nineteen Hundred and Nineteen' until several months later. This is the fourth of his poems for and about Robert Gregory, who had been killed in action in 1918, but whereas Robert's allegiances, in 'An Irish Airman Foresees His Death', for example, had been to his Irish community rather than to the Britain he served, and to his own 'lonely impulse of delight' more than to either, in 'Reprisals' Yeats is asking, surely on his own behalf rather than Robert's, what has gone wrong with the ideal of honour that it seemed could survive even an irrelevant and costly war. Robert died 'a good death'—or 'we' thought he did. At least some people regarded the cause he served as 'a fine affair'. But neither ghost nor man can be satisfied now, Yeats suggests. There is 'other thought' than 'battle joy'. It's not at all clear what has happened, and why the 'today' of the poem is so dire a day.[33]

It is clear that the dead have been cheated by the country they died for—although their 'country', it seems, was perhaps less a nation than a defensible form of civil society represented by 'law and parliament'. This is not a great poem, but its remarkable last lines do great despairing work.

> Some nineteen German planes, they say,
> You had brought down before you died.

---

[33] It's not clear from the poem because of the way a word like 'today' works. But if we take 'today' to be the time of composition, some day in November 1920, it marks a moment right in the midst of Yeats' rising concern about English atrocities in Ireland. I borrow the following details from John Kelly's admirable chronology, *A W. B. Yeats Chronology* (London: Palgrave, 2003). On 22 Aug. 1920, Yeats wrote to Pound saying how much he admired 'Hugh Selwyn Mauberley', with its memorable lines about the war: 'There died a myriad, | And of the best among them, | For an old bitch gone in the teeth, | For a botched civilization'. On 29 Sept. Yeats wrote a letter to *The Times* about the atrocities, and the same day had a conversation with Asquith about them. On 23 Oct. 'Easter 1916' was reprinted in *The New Statesman*. On 15 Jan. 1921 Yeats refused on principle to attend a Warriors Day celebration; on 17 Feb. he denounced British policy at the Oxford Union; and on 5 May he read a version of 'Nineteen Hundred and Nineteen' to Lady Gregory.

We called it a good death. Today
Can ghost or man be satisfied?
Although your last exciting year
Outweighed all other years, you said,
Though battle joy may be so dear
A memory, even to the dead,
It chases other thought away,
Yet rise from your Italian tomb,
Flit to Kiltartan cross and stay
Till certain second thoughts have come
Upon the cause you served, that we
Imagined such a fine affair:
Half-drunk or whole-mad soldiery
Are murdering your tenants there.
Many that revere your father yet
Are shot at on the open plain.
Where may new-married women sit
And suckle children now? Armed men
May murder them in passing by
Nor law nor parliament take heed.
Then close your ears with dust and lie
Among the other cheated dead.[34]

The violence here is not yet the powerful emblem it will become in 'Nineteen Hundred and Nineteen'. Pieces of the picture are already there: 'the cause ... that we | Imagined such a fine affair' looks towards similar lines in the later poem; and the word 'soldiery' itself, mildly archaic, invoking collective behaviour and suggestive of rough off-duty entertainments rather than military

[34] *Variorum Edition*, 791.

action, is already doing some of its work. But there is something wrong with the violence in the poem. It isn't violent enough, or it is merely illustrative. It is happening not to free-standing people but to Robert's tenants and men who revered his father. The women are not individuals who can die but part of a pastoral frieze, maternal presences of picturesque old Ireland, and the poetical-rhetorical question of where they are going to sit and look decorative is close to offensive. It's true that 'may murder them in passing by' is genuinely chilling, and the murmuring m's picked up from 'armed men' do in context suggest something smooth and easy, almost natural. But we are a long way from the horror of the mother murdered at her door and crawling in her own blood.

In the later poem Yeats' recourse is not only to his own considerable poetic powers but to something like the powers of the English language itself. Of course the imagery of crawling in blood is intense, and the repetition of 'her' (her door, her blood) creates a sense of intimate outrage, as does the verb 'leave'—as if the crime were not only to shoot the woman but also to keep going after the shooting, like a driver abandoning the scene of an accident. But the two simple articles—*a* and *the*—do a great deal of the work here, and I am astonished on every reading at how extraordinary that work is. Just reverse the ascriptions and you'll see the nature of the effect: *the* drunken soldiery, *a* murdered mother. No, no, not *the* soldiery, *a* soldiery, any old soldiery and especially the soldiery made of the rag-tag thugs and delinquents who formed the Black and Tans. And not *a* mother, one mother among others, but *the* mother, this mother, someone who is a mother as distinct from being something else. It is possible to allegorize a figure through the definite article, of

course, and Yeats may be seeking to do something of the sort
here. But it isn't possible to lose her, to convert her into a simple
instance, and in this case the allegory would not be at odds with
the specificity of one mother's dying.[35]

There is poignant conundrum attached to this very proposition. Fergus Campbell, as we have seen, calls the dead woman
Ellen Quinn, as do Roy Foster and many other scholars. Lady
Gregory calls her Eileen, and so do more recent commentators, including Helen Vendler. Lucy McDiarmid thinks the
first appellation is an error, a confusion of identities springing
from the fact that Lady Gregory's maid and informant is called
Ellen. This makes good sense, but then The *Galway Observer* for
6 November 1920 opens up the whole question again, since it
calls the murdered woman both Ellen and Eileen.

It may be, of course, that she was Ellen and Eileen, the way
Nelly Dean, in *Wuthering Heights*, is both Ellen and Nelly, but
this is a slender theory and, even if true, would not finally alter
the sense that different women are appearing in the record. It
is as if Eileen or Ellen Quinn can't die in her own person; as if
she gets lost in the uncertainty of history; as if she dies more
intimately in her role as 'the mother' than in any supposedly
more individualized account.

---

[35] In *A Vision* Yeats suggests (twice) a different reading of the effects of the
definite and indefinite article in English. 'An object ... is concrete if I say '*a*
chair, *a* fire', and abstract if I but speak of it as the representative of a class—
'*the* chair, *the* fire', etc.' But he is really interested in the possessive pronoun
('*my* fire, *my* chair'), which he says makes the object 'sensuous'. 'We lose interest', he adds on another page, 'in the abstract and concrete alike' (*A Vision*
(1925), 16, 52). My suggestion is that neither the soldiers nor the mother are
abstract, only concrete in different ways, ragged or focused.

Of course, all deaths are generalized by language, by the very concept of death, and even if we could settle on one name, the event would hardly remain unique, in either of two senses: there will be other Eileens or Ellens, and there will, alas, be other young mothers murdered by drunken soldiers, if not in Ireland then elsewhere, and if not in 1920 then at another time. And yet … Every name and every death belongs to an absolutely specific person, and Rilke's famous prayer that we may all by granted our own deaths can be read in a radically simple way. Rilke's chief suggestion, of course, is that if we are lucky or blessed we shall have a death that answers to our life; but having just one death, our own and no one else's, would also be something. Remembering the detail of this death, this life, while also thinking of others, is a matter for our own active imaginations, and good poems are a help to us in this. They point us to particular times and places, if not always to the time and place literally named in the work.

There is always a riddle about how a poem, or a novel or a play for that matter, can refer to anything, and the very idea of shifting reference is a shifting subject. Helen Vendler writes of the advantage for a poet of 'turning away from the topical and adopting forms of abstraction'.[36] She is right about the topical. It's hard to see how a durable poem could be purely topical, since the topical becomes the arcane as soon as the topic is not in the front of our minds. But Yeats doesn't adopt forms of abstraction, rather the reverse. His language always works through concrete instances rich in complex suggestion, and when he speaks of his 'last symbol' in 'Nineteen Hundred and Nineteen' he means a particular person with a proper name and a home and a date.

[36] *Our Secret Discipline*, 62.

Angela Leighton catches this aspect of Yeats' writing very well in her book *On Form*. His 'similes and metaphors are less figures of speech', she says, 'than figures of literally acted desire ... likenesses are not descriptions, they are events'.[37]

V

I have been talking about a poem called 'Nineteen Hundred and Nineteen' because that is the name it is usually known by, and the name it has in *The Tower*, the place where it first appeared in book form in 1928. If you happen to pick up the very handsome paperback facsimile of this volume, you will get a strong visual sense of the eerie repetition of the name and number. The poem is titled 'Nineteen Hundred and Nineteen', four words, spelled out. At the top of each of nine succeeding pages, as a running header, it has 'Nineteen-Nineteen', two words connected by a hyphen. And after the last words of the poem, in small print, there is a number, four digits: 1919.[38] The title tells the time but hints at magic. It is full of its numerical self; a Platonic idea of a year, if not quite Yeats' Platonic Year. It evokes, as Nicholas Grene wittily says, 'not apocalypse now, but apocalypse tomorrow'.[39]

But when Yeats first published the poem, in *The Dial*, in September 1921 and in *The London Mercury* in November of that year, it wasn't called 'Nineteen Hundred and Nineteen',

---

[37] Angela Leighton, *On Form* (Oxford: Oxford University Press, 2007), 148.

[38] W. B. Yeats, *The Tower: A Facsimile Edition* (New York: Scribner, 2004).

[39] Nicholas Grene, 'Yeats and Dates', in Nicholas Allen and Eve Patten (eds.), *That Island Never Found* (Dublin and Portland: Four Courts Press, 2007), 52.

and in spite of the clear implication of the date at the end of the poem in *The Tower*, it wasn't written in 1919 either—if it had been, it could scarcely have referred, however indirectly, to Mrs Quinn's death in November 1920. The title of the poem for these magazine publications was 'Thoughts upon the Present State of the World'. Roy Foster says the later title is 'confusing'; Terence Brown writes of 'deliberate inaccuracy';[40] and certainly there is more than a little mystification here, a bit of Yeats' fine fraudulence. But there is also more than mystification; a creative 'mistake', let's say, a fiction that is being put to work.[41] The poem still 'refers' to Mrs Quinn if we happen to know about her

---

[40] *The Arch-Poet*, 193. Terence Brown, *The Life of W. B. Yeats* (Oxford: Blackwell, 2001), 317.

[41] Nicholas Grene, in the essay I have just mentioned, distinguishes between 'strategic dating' and 'creative misdating' in Yeats. The first move can create the impression that an earlier poem, 'September 1913', for example, which once knew nothing of the future, was all along 'waiting for "Easter 1916" to be written and complete its meaning'. The second move can be even more startling, since as Grene says, 'every single one of the first four poems in *The Tower* is misdated'—that is, Yeats supplies a false date at the end of each poem as the ostensible date of composition. Perhaps, Grene suggests, Yeats wanted to be seen as covering a larger span of history (1919–1927) than the actual dates of writing (1921–1926) allowed; and certainly, as Grene shrewdly proposes, there is 'a significance in the backward progression of the imagined dates'. The poems are 'Sailing to Byzantium', written 1926, dated 1927; 'The Tower', written 1925, dated 1926; 'Meditations in Time of Civil War', written 1922, dated 1923; and 'Nineteen Hundred and Nineteen', written 1921, dated 1919. 'Each of the poems in this sequence', Grene says, 'takes off from the previous one, undoing what the previous poem has seemed to close off' (ibid. 48). We should note too that only 'Nineteen Hundred and Nineteen' is dated earlier rather than later than its time of composition; and it is the only poem in the sequence whose title is a date. It is the only poem in Yeats' whole work whose title is simply a year.

murder, even if the thing is now literally impossible in terms of what the page of the book is telling us. And it wouldn't 'refer' to her anyway if we didn't know who she was. The trick of the poem in its later incarnation is to specify a time that represents a still real but no longer literal history. The challenge for readers is to hang on to the specifics even when they are multiple, not to let actual if mobile times and places slip away into symbols and lazy universals. David Hume in the *Treatise* reminds us 'that the imagination is more affected by what is particular, than by what is general; and that the sentiments are always moved with difficulty, where their objects are, in any degree, loose and undetermined'.[42] My argument is that a poem can be historically fixed in different ways, by its origins, by its ostensible or occluded points of reference, and by the connections its readers choose to make; that these are different modes of connection to the real world; and that all of these connections can be 'loose or undetermined', although none of them has to be.

'Nineteen Hundred and Nineteen' as a title evokes an array of times and places for us, sets us a sort of puzzle in a way that 'the present state of the world' doesn't. What do we find in that named year, in our memories and encyclopaedias and histories? We find Ireland, of course, and specifically the Ireland of the revolution, caught between the Rising and the Civil War. In January 1919 two members of the Royal Irish Constabulary were killed in Tipperary, an event 'generally taken to have

---

[42] David Hume, *A Treatise of Human Nature* (Oxford: Oxford University Press, 1978), 580. Quoted in Michael Bell, *Sentimentalism, Ethics and the Culture of Feeling* (Basingstoke: Palgrave, 2000), 41.

opened hostilities', Charles Townsend says, 'in what has come to be called the Irish War of Independence'.[43] The first Dail Eireann met in the Mansion House in Dublin in January, the Black and Tans were first despatched in February. Also in February, creating one of the stories that haunted my Lincoln childhood because it was still part of the local stock of fabulous deeds, Eamon de Valera escaped from Lincoln Prison. In 1919 most Irish Volunteer units adopted a new title: the Irish Republican Army. The Civil War in Russia was two years old and still had three or four years to go. Roy Foster tells us that in the summer of 1919 Yeats 'wrote to AE pointing out that Russian communists had killed not 400 but 13,000 people'.[44] We can think also of the unsettled and disappointing landscape represented by the Treaty of Versailles, signed in June 1919. And our thoughts, if not those of Yeats, might well associate 1919 with the Spartacist uprising in Germany, the deaths of Rosa Luxemburg and Karl Liebknecht, the short-lived Bavarian Socialist Republic and the massacre at the Sikh temple in Amritsar, all certainly part of the history of violence. In other but perhaps not unrelated realms of theory and practice, 1919 was also the year of Freud's essay on the uncanny, Robert Wiene's film *The Cabinet of Dr Caligari,* and Max Weber's lecture in Munich—'in the revolutionary winter of 1919'—on politics as a vocation, where he explained, among other things, that violence (*Gewaltsamkeit,* literally forcefulness) was 'of course not anything like

[43] Charles Townshend, *Ireland: the 20th Century* (London: Arnold, 1999), 87.
[44] *The Arch-Poet,* 147.

the normal or only means of the state ... but nevertheless the means specific to it'.[45]

This is all worth thinking about, but the internal movements of the poem give us a more secure location: a mentality that is itself a densely populated time and place, and in this sense the 'now' of the poem, the 'present' of the early title and the 'Nineteen Hundred and Nineteen' of the later one do not need to be minutely distinguished from each other, because the mentality is so deep and durable and angry at its own errors. The 'seven years ago' mentioned in the poem may take us back to 1914 or to 1912 but both years belong irrecoverably to the *then* that *now* has turned into a regrettable and foolish fantasy.

Yeats said on re-reading *The Tower* that he was 'astonished at its bitterness',[46] and we can understand his astonishment—because the bitterness is caught up in an extraordinarily vivid, almost exhilarating range of wit. But we can't mistake the tone, any more than he did. He has become one of those 'bitter and violent men' he writes about in another poem in *The Tower*, the rich men, architects and artists who create, or have created for them, the historical antonyms to their own temperaments and times, the sweetness and gentleness they have never known. Except that here, in the present state of the world, there is no sweetness or gentleness, and the very idea of such moods, even in art, looks like folly.

---

[45] Max Weber, *Politik als Beruf* (Munich and Leipzig: Duneker and Humblot, 1926), 8. My translation.

[46] Letter to Olivia Shakespear, 25 April 1928, cited in *The Tower*, xii.

VI

'The plunge of civilisation into this abyss of blood and darkness', Henry James wrote in a letter when the First World War began, 'so gives away the whole long age during which we have supposed the world to be, with whatever abatement, gradually bettering, that to have to take it now for what the treacherous years were all the while really making for and meaning is too tragic for any words.'[47] I'll return in a moment to an identification of the 'we' who were doing this strange supposing, a group closely related to the 'we' who are arraigned in the Yeats poem, although the anger the poem so energetically articulates produces a very different tone from James' melancholy sense of betrayal.

Towards the end of Part I of the poem we meet what appears to be a timeless, and lovely, piece of verse, a proposition not inflected by anger or a sense of folly, and announcing what looks like the 'theme' of this poem as of many other poems by Yeats and others: 'Man is in love and loves what vanishes, | What more is there to say?' There is nothing more to say, it seems. There is only the perfect and always necessary saying again, as in Horace, or Ovid, or Virgil, or Villon, or Shakespeare: there are tears for things, there is the continuing engulfment of everything in time. But of course there is more to say, and a good deal of it has already been said in this poem. There are questions to ask. What was it we loved, and why did it vanish? Because everything vanishes? No need to get so excited then. But is this

---

[47] Henry James, letter to Howard Sturgis, quoted in F. W. Dupee, *Henry James* (New York: Delta, 1965), 248–9.

what civilization is, and is this why we lost it? Yeats often suggests as much, in 'Lapis Lazuli', for example, and no doubt often believes in the claim. We can believe in it too, maybe, in the long view. But in the immediate context of the lively, complex shifting tone and meanings of this poem, the long view looks like an attempt at self-consolation, beautifully disguised as mourning. If all we had to do was mourn, the suggestion is, we could be calmly sorrowful; we could just mourn. And our shock and bitterness and blame would have vanished, like the objects of our love, into a kind of eternity of loss.

In fact, the whole of the first part of 'Nineteen Hundred and Nineteen' invites us to a double reading, or tells two stories, the first about loss, the second about the folly of our believing we ever had what we think we have lost. Here's how the story of loss goes: 'Many ingenious (or ingenuous, I'll come back to this) lovely things are gone ...'; 'We too had many pretty toys when young ...'; 'All teeth were drawn, all ancient tricks unlearned ...'; 'We pieced our thoughts into philosophy ...' But now we know, since the hour of truth has come round at last, that 'no work can stand, | Whether health, wealth or peace of mind were spent | On master-work of intellect or hand, | No honour leave its mighty monument'. From here the step to generalized mourning is not a long one: we love what vanishes and it was never, in the end, going to do anything but vanish.

But the speaker of the poem, as Michael Ragussis very well says, 'refuses the solace of sorrow'.[48] The other story is altogether

---

[48] Michael Ragussis, *The Subterfuge of Art* (Baltimore: Johns Hopkins University Press, 1978), 94.

more troubling, and has to do with very subtle shifts of object and forms of illustration. To start with, the difference between 'ingenious' and 'ingenuous', in this context, is much smaller than it might be elsewhere. I don't really doubt that 'ingenuous', as the word appears in *The Dial*, is the misprint most scholars think it is, but then it's a fortunate slip, a sort of Freudian message from the printer's font. The 'things' that are gone are cleverly or innocently made, they are not mighty monuments. The Parthenon, for example, may be a ruin but it's still there. The ingenious lovely things are the reverse of monuments: fragile instances of the art of an ancient time, a statue made from an olive tree, carved ivories, grasshoppers and bees made of gold. These things lasted, not forever, but for a spell, because they were, it seems, magically protected 'from the circle of the moon | That pitches common things about'. They were delicate and lovely, and the surprise is not that they are gone, but that they should have lasted beyond their own cultural moment at all. There is cause for sorrow here, but no reason to be shocked; we love fragile things, and fragile things get broken, what more is there to say?

What there is to say is what follows when Yeats moves from delicate art objects to the forms of civil life. 'We too had many pretty toys when young', he says. There is already something amiss in the phrase 'pretty toys', since surely the ancient ivories and the rest were a little more than that, and the elegantly trivializing term looks like a gesture of self-protection: these were bearable losses, a matter of civilization's infancy—and perhaps the meaning of 'ingenuous' come back here. But there is worse to come. What are these toys? The rule of law, lack of corruption, habits of justice, a society informed by a mature public opinion. Toys? Yes, because we didn't have them, only their simulacra; we had only the illusion of having them.

'O what fine thought we had because we thought | That the worst rogues and rascals had died out.' It's worth lingering over the double meaning created by the line-break. 'O what fine thought we had because we thought' and 'O what fine thought we had because we thought that the worst rogues and rascals had died out.' The particular thought was deluded, certainly, but perhaps thinking itself is delusion. Or at least can seem so when you are in the mood this speaker is in. We might believe that the continuing presence of rogues and rascals, even of 'the worst' rogues and rascals, is a feature of social reality, and that the law exists precisely to protect ordinary citizens from them. How could anyone have thought they would have died out? But that was just what our 'fine thought' was: the law was 'indifferent to blame or praise, | To bribe or threat', because it was a dream of law, an imaginary, untested law, a law for a world without rogues and rascals. A good deal of the anger of the poem arises from the sudden and total awareness of this error. Not: did we believe what we believed, but: how could we?

The next stanza redescribes the error in grimly comic terms. The terms are grim because the violence that has shocked us so was there all the time, but we thought it had become a game, a matter of toys, 'a great army but a showy thing'. A. N. Jeffares reminds us of a speech Yeats gave in 1924 recalling a friend's comment made two weeks before war broke out in 1914 about the 'fine sight' of an English military parade. A Member of Parliament standing next to this friend said, 'It is a fine sight, but it is nothing else, there will never be another war.'[49] And the terms are comic because the lines from Isaiah about learning war no more, and beating swords into ploughshares, are given a modern, ceremonial rendering. We haven't turned our cannons into ploughshares, but not because we are still learning war; only because we like the imagery of war. In Yeats' bitter and oblique irony, we kept our weapons because our rituals needed them, because trumpeting without gunshot lacks glory and because the guardsmen's horses might sleep through their parades if they were not challenged by at least the noises of violent conflict.

But these horses were never asleep, and they instantly make a strange double appearance—as riders rather than ridden, and as dragons rather than horses ... These animals assume a strange, blurry form—linguistically blurry, I mean. Of course 'ridden' is the past participle of the verb 'to ride', but 'dragon-ridden' sounds more like 'hag-ridden' than anything else—the OED also gives us priest-ridden, devil-ridden, and king-ridden, with a meaning of 'oppressed, taken advantage of', described as obsolete. The dragons are haunting us, persecuting us but not literally riding our days. And yet no sooner do we make this slight move away from the literal than the word 'rides' returns, now in connection with a nightmare, which may or may not have an equine connection etymologically—no flicker of a horse in the French cauchemar, for example—but in this sequence can't escape the association. The language, seemingly direct, becomes

---

[49] A. N. Jeffares, *A New Commentary on the Poems of W. B. Yeats* (Stanford: Stanford University Press, 1984), 231. The whole passage is quoted in Grene, 'Yeats and Dates'.

slightly opaque, a very characteristic Yeats effect, and the presence/absence of riding, the horse that is not a horse make us feel the horror is both unshakeable and slightly out of focus. Not for long, because we instantly see the drunken soldiery and the murdered mother in her blood. This is not a nightmare, but a source of nightmare, and the next four lines bring together and say clearly what the poem has been hinting at and exercising its grim and angry wit on:

> The night can sweat with terror as before
> We pieced our thoughts into philosophy
> And planned to bring the world under a rule
> Who are but weasels fighting in a hole.

The 'we' here indicts everyone who shared or even abetted the illusion, from poets to statesmen to well-intentioned parents, not only those who pieced together the philosophy or counted on doing the ruling, but also those who didn't take the trouble to contradict the illusion they knew was wrong: all the weasels who paraded as humanitarians or complacently watched the parade.

The next stanza offers an apparent non sequitur—also very characteristic of Yeats, as are real non sequiturs—driven in this case, it seems, by the need to think a different range of thoughts. Yeats turns to a solitary third person, a 'he who' looks at this mess and draws his conclusions, which point us to the story of loss I have already described. This man, rejecting the recourse to 'some intoxicant', has 'but one comfort left', and a very curious one at that: 'all triumph would | But break upon his ghostly solitude'. We may feel we liked him better when he was railing—if so, we can be reassured, for he soon starts railing again, and more and more bitterly. But what is he saying here? That it doesn't matter if projects fail because they were in any case a mere interruption of the haughty spirit of lonely inaction? A sort of modern version of the Sophoclean claim that 'never to have lived is best', as Yeats puts it in his translation of a chorus from *Oedipus at Colonus*—and if we can't manage that, then not to act is the next best thing. The delicate irony here is that the speaker genuinely seems to want his ghostly solitude, which Yeats writes about beautifully elsewhere; but knows he can't return to it, and that it wouldn't be a comfort if he could.

In its final stanza, Part I of the poem plays its best, almost winning card: the story of loss I evoked earlier. And yet no sooner does our elegist ask 'What more is there to say?' than he is saying something else. He is telling a story of destruction and theft—or rather craftily pretending that such things used not to be possible, and more craftily still, pretending that even if they were possible no one would admit they were possible.

> That country round
> None dared admit, if such a thought were his,
> Incendiary or bigot could be found
> To burn that stump on the Acropolis,
> Or break in bits the famous ivories
> Or traffic in the grasshoppers or bees.

We have to ask how far this old *then* finally is from the recently described *now*. Just what is the difference between refusing to admit the thought that incendiaries and bigots can be found and indulging in the belief that the worst rascals and rogues have died out? There is a difference, of course, but it isn't that what has happened now couldn't have happened then. It is that they can't admit what might happen and we have been forced to admit that almost anything can happen again. The movement from destruction to trafficking makes the charge particularly scathing. Many ingenious lovely things could find their way on to the black market: the indignity seems below pathos.

VII

I promised to return to the 'we' who supposed the world to be gradually bettering, who had such fine thought and dreamed of mending mischief:

> O but we dreamed to mend
> Whatever mischief seemed
> To afflict mankind, but now
> That winds of winter blow
> Learn that we were crack-pated when we dreamed.

The appeal to the dream has all kinds of echoes in Yeats, and what happens here represents an important change. We might think the dream justifies the dreamer, since that is part of the argument of 'Easter 1916', and this is the argument the speaker of 'Nineteen Hundred and Nineteen' helplessly gestures towards: 'We know their dream', the earlier poem says, 'enough | To know they dreamed and are dead'. This particular dream had its price, even apart from the death of the dreamers. It turned hearts to stone, as I have already mentioned, it was part of the old myth of sacrifice Yeats himself used to be so eloquent about. But it also changed the world, and took the dreamers out of 'the casual comedy' that seemed to be their life, associating them with a 'terrible beauty' that hindsight could only enhance, not undo. The crack-pated dreamers of 'Nineteen Hundred and Nineteen' by contrast are ruined by hindsight, they were only dreaming, and it is not 'enough | To know they dreamed', and not just because they are not all dead yet. Even death will not convert their errors into anything but folly. But why is this? And who are they?

They are a class, as Roy Foster says, the old Ascendancy in Ireland. Elsewhere Yeats borrows a phrase from the poem to talk about Lady Gregory, who is said to be 'indifferent to praise or blame',[50] a quality attributed to the law that was one of the pretty toys 'we' had when young. But then our youth in this sense goes back a while, at least to the eighteenth century, as Foster suggests, and by the early twentieth century that class was nervous rather than idealistic, and many Protestants were arming rather than dreaming. Foster also invokes England and the Pax Britannica, and I think Yeats, like James, is skilfully creating a kind of movable moral and political community, English, Irish, American, a now-defunct club to which anyone who was wrong about the world can claim to have belonged. Or can be accused, by themselves or others, of having belonged to. Members would be, for instance, all the casualties of what George Dangerfield long ago called the strange death of liberal England; all Irish people who hoped for a non-violent progression to independence; all cosmopolitan Americans, from the north or the south

---

[50] *Autobiographies*, 286.

of the continent, who thought of themselves as belonging to an international civilization; and in the club's most capacious definition, all the inheritors of the Enlightenment, in Europe and across the world, all the believers in some sort of moral progress running alongside the nineteenth century's manifest advances in science and technology.

Did such a club exist, except in a retrospective arrangement, to borrow a phrase from Joyce? This is hard to say, since the evidence comes mostly from the club's repentant and guilty members, in instances full of self-parody. Of course people did say, and perhaps believe, that war was a thing of the past, and politicians spoke of putting an end to poverty. This is still some way from believing that the worst rogues and rascals have died out. There is a difference, surely, between a dream as an ideal or a programme and a dream as a damaging, and once revealed as such, shocking delusion. And yet the shock is what seems to have been most real in all this, and what cries out for interpretation. Historians can argue, we can all argue about whether the world was 'gradually bettering' in the later Victorian era—medicine will tell us a quite different story from politics, and certain classes of Belle Époque France, say, were doing very nicely compared to Russian serfs—and we can argue philosophically about whether the idea of the moral improvement of a whole civilization is even coherent. But what James and Yeats are showing us is not how things were but how they dramatically felt, and they had many companions in this feeling. Ezra Pound, for example, in 'Hugh Selwyn Mauberley' (1920), but here is a subtler case.

John Dowell, the narrator of Ford Madox Ford's *The Good Soldier* (1915) is trying to tell us about his wife's infidelity and his friend's unhappiness, but he sounds as if he is talking about a whole culture.

> Permanence? Stability? I can't believe it's gone. I can't believe that that long, tranquil life, which was just stepping a minuet, vanished in four crashing days at the end of nine years and six weeks.
> And yet I swear by the sacred name of my creator that it was true. It was true sunshine; the true music; the true splash of the fountains from the mouth of stone dolphins.
> If for nine years I have possessed a goodly apple that is rotten at the core and discover its rottenness only in nine years and six months less four days, isn't it true to say that for nine years I possessed a goodly apple?[51]

The answer is no: the apple was rotten at the core, no doubt about it. But of course the feeling of possessing a goodly apple may have been real enough too. What matters here, what drives the novel and cannot be exorcized, is not the actual or imagined state of the apple, but the news about the apple's condition, the outrageous information that Dowell cannot lay hold of mentally, to lift a phrase from Ford's friend Joseph Conrad. And this is the story we are looking at in Yeats and James: the historical moment is neither now nor then but the moment formed by what *now* is seen as doing to *then*. Better: by what a particular emblematic feature of *now* is doing to the whole of *then*. If the Magi were waiting for a turbulence they knew was coming, the contemporaries of our writers are like Magi who have lost the plot, or rather found a plot they had in no way looked for.

---

[51] Ford Madox Ford, *The Good Soldier* (Oxford: Oxford University Press, 1990), 10–11.

For James as for Pound as for many others the desolating new plot centres on the war or rather the instigation of war, what James calls 'the wanton feat of those two infamous autocrats'. Yeats felt differently about this instance. 'It is merely the most expensive outbreak of insolence and stupidity the world has ever seen', he wrote to John Quinn in New York, and he told Henry James he was determined to lie low 'till bloody frivolity is over'.[52] He didn't entirely lie low—he sent a poem to Edith Wharton for her *Book of the Homeless*, in aid of two refugee charities, and he took part in a reading for Belgian relief—but clearly it wasn't the war, however expensive, insolent, and stupid it was, that taught him to think differently about the age supposedly without rogues and rascals. The war for Yeats was 'merely' a new highpoint in what the world was used to seeing. I don't think the Black and Tans changed Yeats' mind either, or not on their own. The shift was no doubt cumulative, starting perhaps with his understanding of what had happened at Easter 1916, and including his reluctant recognition that 'England may be criminal enough to grant to violence what she refused to reason'.[53] But the drunken soldiery were his emblem, not the European war; a double emblem, because they were murderers and because they went scot-free.

If the new understanding evoked by James and Yeats doesn't literally arrive through violence, although perhaps for James it does, they both picture the breaking of illusion as having violence at its heart, and indeed possible only through violence. The picture doesn't make this or any other violence acceptable or welcome, but it does mean that no one can deny or even deplore the new truth, because the truth is always in one respect an improvement on fantasy—in one respect only, I hasten to add, since fantasy is an improvement on truth in every other way, that is what fantasy is for. Still, this respect is important. One can't build on error, and with truth there is at least a chance.

At the same time this new understanding so completely wrecks the past that for the moment the wreck is all that can be seen, as Ford's narrator can see only the breaking news, not the past or present story. Violence, I want to say, is the name of this wreck; it is whatever brings to our minds the knowledge we cannot and will not gain otherwise. It would be desperate and in a horrible way romantic to believe that there just is no other way in which we can get the knowledge we need, and we should certainly try to do without uncontrollable mysteries if we can. But I also think we should listen to what Yeats and others are saying, to what Yeats is saying better than any other, to what his precision, his wit, his anger, his images, his rhythms, his off-rhymes and his sheer unflagging attention to the vanishing world have to tell us: once days are dragon-ridden, however we explain the arrival of the dragon, neither the past nor the future can be the same.

2

The Platonic Year

'I do not want to concern myself, except where I must, with political events'

W. B. YEATS, *A Vision* (1925)

'Somehow you arranged your escape
Aboard a spirit ship which every day
Hoisted sail out of fire and rape'

EAVAN BOLAND, *'Yeats
in Civil War'*

I

There are various forms of time at work in Part I of 'Nineteen Hundred and Nineteen': the thematic year of the title; the year of the poem's composition and publication; the deluded age of pre-war optimism; the remote and celebrated centuries of ancient Greece; the timeless time of human affection for what vanishes. But there is no mention in this part of the poem—there is just one in the whole work, and another in Yeats' note—of the time that mattered most to the poet for much of his life: the long, 'sidereal' time of his metaphysical system, of his scheme of other worlds and other lives, the effect of his patient quest for conversations with the dead. This is often the time of the dance for Yeats, rhythmic, composed, magical, transcendental. In *A Vision* 'some great dancer' is offered to us as 'the perfect flower of modern culture'. And when Yeats pictures Salome 'dancing before Herod', he invites us to 'wonder if what seems to us decadence was not in reality the exaltation of the muscular flesh and of civilisation perfectly achieved'. A rather violent perfection, to be sure, since Salome is about to receive 'the Prophet's head in her indifferent hands', but then Yeats is thinking about revelation, or more precisely, 'the moment before revelation'.[1]

In Part II of 'Nineteen Hundred and Nineteen', Yeats' metaphysical time makes its appearance as a dance; but the dance becomes an image not of art or perfection but of helplessness. It is not a question, as it is in 'Among School Children', another poem in *The Tower*, of whether we can tell the dancer from the dance but whether we can see anything of the dancer but her name and her most famous device. What we are shown are the great billowing sheets of silk Loie Fuller spun wildly around herself at great speed, as if she were simultaneously engineering a great storm and dangerously caught up in it.

> When Loie Fuller's Chinese dancers enwound
> A shining web, a floating ribbon of cloth,
> It seemed that a dragon of air
> Had fallen among dancers, had whirled them round
> Or hurried them off on its own furious path.

[1] W. B. Yeats, *A Vision (1938)* (New York: Macmillan, 1961), 240, 271.

Commentators like to point out that Fuller's dancers were Japanese rather than Chinese, but it seems unlikely that Yeats, who could be casual about many things, was making a mistake here. He knew a lot about Japanese culture, and after all the dancers weren't waving their passports. 'Chinese' here, I think, like 'gong' later, invokes an ancient Far East rather than a distinct nationality. You could be a Chinese dancer even if you were Japanese—or American, as Loie Fuller was.

There are a number of remarkable images of Fuller's dance in her clouds of silk—a painting by Toulouse Lautrec, a famous poster, several fine old photographs. All of these, though, suggest something rather ethereal about the performance, a woman caught up in wisps of air and colour. Frank Kermode uses a wonderful drawing of Loie Fuller by Thomas Theodor Heine as 'the best visual illustration [he] could find' for his thoughts about Yeats and the dance, and he is certainly right if we think of Yeats' dancers more broadly.[2] The tall, slender figure is all *Art Nouveau*. But if we look at the Lumière Brothers' brief film,[3] made in 1897, of Fuller's much performed (and much imitated) 'danse serpentine', her snake dance, or snake-style dance, we see something different, and closer to the effect Yeats is evoking in 'Nineteen Hundred and Nineteen'—although he characteristically turns the snake into a dragon, so that her show, like the present state of the world, becomes dragon-ridden. The film has been tinted, and the colours of the silks change all the time,

[2] Frank Kermode, *Romantic Image* (New York: Vintage, 1964), note on frontispiece.

[3] As YouTube now permits us easily to do.

from brown to yellow to pink to white, and so on—a trick Fuller could hardly have pulled off on the stage without a change of kit. This is distracting, and of course picks up the colour theme from painting and poster. But what finally stays in the mind after viewing this amazing piece of early cinema is the sheer rabid energy of the whirl of silks, the way they dwarf the tiny whirler, and how often she disappears from view into the material of her own practice. It's as if she keeps getting eaten by a dragon of air, or at least of millinery.

The rhetorical form of Part II of the poem is the extended simile, a single sentence that first describes Fuller's dance, then likens it to the movement of the Platonic year and concludes with an aphoristic summary bringing together the pieces of the comparison:

> So the Platonic year
> Whirls out new right and wrong,
> Whirls in the old instead;
> All men are dancers and their tread
> Goes to the barbarous clangour of a gong.

The early editions had 'the barbarous clangour of gong', which is slightly awkward but also powerful, since it makes the sound accompanying the universal dance both more exotic and more generic. The simile works both ways, forwards and backwards, like Yeats' 'double vortex'.[4] The movement of the Platonic year is like that of the serpentine dance, and the movement of the dance is like that of the Platonic year. There is an asymmetry in

---

[4] *A Vision (1938)*, 197, 209, 210.

the reversal, though. Human beings in time are like dancers on a historical stage; and on another, eternal stage the dancers are dancers twice over, once literally as themselves and once metaphorically like everyone else.

What is striking here, what tells us so much about this poem and its place in Yeats' work and life, is how unavailing the symbolic scheme of *A Vision* is at this point of historical anxiety. All it suggests here is a grim determinism, an oriental march of fate. We see nothing of the elaborate poetry of Yeats' system, the endless variables and the brilliant examples which make the whole pattern anything but predetermined: we could always be in phase or out of phase, choose our true mask or false mask, redeem or mess up our lives in countless ways, even within the 'mathematical necessity' of the whole vast mythology.[5]

In 'Nineteen Hundred and Nineteen' the idea of cyclical change just means more of the same: new right and wrong are whirled out and the old team is whirled in to take their place. In *A Vision* Yeats is very keen to avoid what he saw as Vico's error, which was 'to suggest … civilisation perpetually returning to the same point'; but it's very hard to read the lines in the poem as suggesting anything else.[6] It's telling that the new should go and the old come back, rather than the old finally giving place to the new, so the magical circuits are at least good for an angry paradox. But

[5] W. B. Yeats, *A Vision: The Original 1925 Version*, ed. Catherine E. Paul and Margaret Mills Harper (New York: Scribner, 2008), lvii.

[6] *A Vision (1938)*, 255. Cf. Graham Hough, *The Mystery Religion of W. B. Yeats* (Brighton: Harvester, 1984), 117: 'Yeats was haunted by determinism—partly fascinated and partly repelled, as he was by the era of violence he foresaw for the world in the next cycle.'

there is no art or freedom or hope in either half of the comparison. In spite of the poet's reaching for a different world, for the other world that meant so much to him in the time before and after the writing of this poem, we are still in the mood of Part I. The whole beautiful system, with its redemption of reality and justice, is entirely subjected to the interpretative powers of the weasels: dragon, clangour, barbarism, and the rhyming of gong with wrong, the bad old times returning. The delicate promise momentarily held out by the notion of the dance and the 'shining web' and the 'floating ribbon' is just that: a promise no sooner intimated than gone. Perhaps the strange word 'enwound' already poisoned or snagged the promise a little.

II

The Platonic Year, or the Great Year, is a traditional name for the period in which all the planets and fixed stars complete a cycle and return to a configuration they have occupied before, some 26,000 years according to the calculation Yeats is using—his instructors, he said, meaning the spirits who spoke to him through his wife, 'have ... adopted the twenty-six thousand years of modern astronomy instead of the thirty-six thousand years Spenser [in *The Faerie Queene*] took from the Platonic Year'.[7] This Year could be divided into twelve 'months' that became for Yeats the spells of two thousand plus years between catastrophic historical incarnations. Such a month would in turn have its months, and every division, including what we ordinarily call a

---

[7] *A Vision (1938)*, 202.

calendar year, would have its seasons and phases of the moon, and would allow us to think, at the most immediate level, of what Yeats calls a 'symbolical or ideal year', incredibly long or reasonably short, 'each month a brightening and a darkening fortnight, and at the same time perhaps a year with its four seasons'.[8] The pattern runs all the way through the different levels and dimensions ('every period of time is both a month and year'[9]), and it's easy to see how the Platonic Year could become for Yeats an emblem of remote but undeniable regularity, and a figure for whatever there is that ultimately, however belatedly and at whatever cost, refutes randomness and asserts the enduring principle of order, or perhaps simply of the possibility of such a principle.

The ancient world, Yeats says, engaged in 'an acceptance or half acceptance of that Year, not for its astronomical but for its moral value'. Plato, he suggests, is stuck with a conception of the Great Year 'which five minutes arithmetic would have refuted', but uses the frame 'as we use the lunar phases, as if it were the moving hands upon a vast clock, or a picturesque symbolism that helped him to make more vivid and perhaps date, developments of the human mind that can be proved dialectically'.[10] This intriguing picture, a symbol of symbolism, no doubt tells us more about Yeats than about Plato, but it helps us with the myth-making of both, since it marks the moment when mathematical calculations part company with other modes of truth-telling. 'Make vivid and perhaps date developments of the human mind': this curiously modest and extraordinarily ambitious enterprise is precisely what Yeats is

---

[8] *A Vision (1938)*, 196, 246.   [9] Ibid., 251.
[10] *A Vision (1925)*, 123, 125–6.

pursuing in *A Vision*, and it is what he evokes in his grandest statements about his system and what it did for him. It made him feel, he wrote to Lady Gregory in January 1918, 'that for the first time I understand human life'.[11] Once he connects his numbers with his diagrams, he says in his second version of the text itself, he will 'possess a classification ... of every possible movement of thought and life'.[12] These are surely expressions of extreme excitement and enthusiasm rather than claims of philosophical or taxonomical triumph. Their interest for us lies in what they tell us about Yeats' intellectual appetite, about what he wants from knowledge. To feel one understands human life and possesses a vast classification of it is not the same as committing particular acts of understanding and classifying, any of which could be wrong without falsifying the intuition of a more general rightness.

This is the perspective that 'Nineteen Hundred and Nineteen' cannot reach, and Yeats himself was fully aware of a secession from his 'philosophy'. He told Olivia Shakespear in a letter written in April 1921 that he was at work on 'a series of poems ('Thoughts suggested by the present state of the world' or some such name). I have written two and there may be many more'. There were four more, as we know, since the poem 'Nineteen Hundred and Nineteen' is made up of six 'poems'. The series, Yeats said, was 'a lamentation over lost peace and lost hope. My own philosophy does not much brighten the prospect'.[13] It is

---

[11] Quoted in Introduction to *A Vision (1925)*, xxxi.

[12] *A Vision (1938)*, 78.

[13] Quoted in George Mills Harper, *The Making of Yeats's A Vision* (New York: Macmillan, 1987), vol. 2: 399.

strange to hear Yeats strike this note in relation to his visionary scheme, since his philosophy usually does, albeit in very complicated ways, 'brighten the prospect'. Perhaps his spirit ship just wouldn't sail in 'the present state of the world'?

But it did, or rather it had completed most of its voyages, and the captain was back in port reviewing the log. And in any case Yeats' intense traffic with the spirits over the years 1917 to 1920 was not an escape from historical reality. It was a patient, even pedantic search for that reality's better self. Yeats called it 'a last act of defence against the chaos of the world', and added 'I hope for ten years to write out of my renewed security'.[14] He said this in 1925—and so had forgotten, it seems, the vanishing of this security in 1921. Did it vanish for the space of only one poem or only one season? As I have suggested, the sense that his 'philosophy' was of no avail at all to anyone in the historical mood evoked in 'Nineteen Hundred and Nineteen' does indeed place the poem in a special region of Yeats' work. But I must add immediately that the poem itself offers an urgent commentary on the philosophy it can't use; and that the philosophy is littered with conscientiously construed doubts and difficulties. It is a defence against chaos, not a defeat of chaos. Chaos, at any given moment, is always likely to win, and the question, for the system and for virtually any poem, is about degrees and styles and effects of defence.

It is worth remembering too that 1919, the symbolic year of the poem, and 1921, the year of its composition, represented quite different moments in the world and especially in Ireland.

---

[14] Letter quoted in *The Making of Yeats's A Vision*, vol. 2: 407–8.

Indeed, writing to Lady Gregory at about the same time as he wrote to Olivia Shakespear, Yeats mentioned a poem 'on the state of things in Ireland', rather than 'the present state of the world'.[15] In 1919, with the European war over, what had been an increasingly violent series of clashes between Irish guerrillas and English policemen became a war between countries. The shift of terms was itself a victory for the Nationalists, and the ineptness and cruelty of the English government's responses to unrest formed one of the most persuasive arguments yet for independence. In July 1921 a truce was declared in what everyone now called the Anglo-Irish War (Yeats published his poem in September), and a peace treaty, debated in December, was narrowly ratified in January 1922. The closeness of the call effectively unleashed the Irish Civil War. We could also add the so-to-speak phantom year 1920, when the literal referent for the drunken soldiery was in action in the West of Ireland. Three moments: three different challenges for whatever understanding the captain and crew of the spirit ship have to offer us.

This understanding is not a refusal of violence but a framing of violence, and the terms that are so scarce in Yeats' poems are everywhere in *A Vision*. An ancient woodcut of the Great Wheel that appears in both editions has *Violentia* as one of its cardinal points, placed where the moon is half dark, half light. Its counterpart, also half dark, half light, is *Temptatio*, while the full moon is *Pulchritudo*, and the full dark is *Sapientia*. Arabs are known 'for the

---

[15] Quoted in Nicholas Grene, 'Yeats and Dates', in Nicholas Allan and Eve Patten (eds.), *That Island Never Found* (Dublin and Portland, Oregon: Four Courts Press, 2007), 46.

violent contrasts of character among them'. We are asked to imagine 'a dissolving violent phantom'. The Will may assert itself 'with a savage, terrified violence'. 'A new birth ... is sometimes so violent that ... it forestalls its ultimate destiny'. A man turns 'violently from all sensual pleasure', another 'gives himself to violent animal assertion', yet another is 'fragmentary and violent'. There are people (like Landor) who are 'violent in themselves' while others are 'violent in their intellect'. A man of a certain phase may 'become a destroyer and persecutor, a figure of tumult and violence'; a man of the next phase is 'violent, anarchic'. There is 'a phase of violent scattering', or 'violent scattering energy'. Some violence—but only some—'seems accidental, unforeseen and cruel'. Yeats thinks of 'the gusts of sentimentality that overtake violent men', sees in Wilde 'much that is violent, arbitrary and insolent'. At certain historical moments 'violent men, each master of some generalisation, arise one after another', and the symbolic gyres may themselves be violent. A spirit before birth may see the 'events and people that shall influence its coming life upon earth' and consequently find itself 'possessed with violent love and hate'.[16]

At one point Yeats asked his spirit instructors rather cryptically 'Ezra of violence, Nietzsche violence?' but didn't get a reply.[17] We may read his own answer perhaps in a rejected passage which tells us that the inheritors of the new world, namely 'all those who have resisted or suffered defeat in the defence of some rank, physiological or intellectual, which has sought its

---

[16] *A Vision* (1925), lx, 19, 46, 35–6, 52, 18, 78, 80, 56, 60, 58, 76, 69, 171, 170, 195–6.
[17] Ibid. 250.

own expression ... all who thirst for whatever is hierarchical and distinguished', will have to be 'young and confident ... and violent because those spiritual energies that have come down from the Sermon on the Mount, through the impersonality of our empirical sciences are now exhausted'.[18] This is Nietzscheanism of a very particular stripe, and it's somewhere around here that Mussolini slouches towards Rome to be born. Yeats told Pound, himself described in an early draft of *A Vision* as 'a very violent talker', that the work was going to be 'full of my sort of violence and passion'. He wasn't exaggerating.[19]

Obviously, as this little anthology suggests, violence means many things to Yeats. However, the same evidence makes clear that he was prepared, even eager to talk about it and that the turbulence depicted in 'Nineteen Hundred and Nineteen' cannot have been what made his philosophy so unavailing there. What ruined the prospect and almost yielded victory to chaos was not anything the world was doing, but the absence of any alternative to sour disappointment and mockery. The poem shows a generation and a culture entirely given over to unbelief. Yeats can't imagine anything worse; and for the moment can't imagine anything better.

His other mention of the Platonic Year in relation to 'Nineteen Hundred and Nineteen' ends his note about Robert Artisson and his activities in fourteenth-century Kilkenny: 'Are not those who travel in the whirling dust also in the Platonic Year?' Here there is more of an opening to the philosophy, and the action of whirling, whatever frightful figures it brings into view, is not just a

---

[18] Ibid. 317.   [19] Ibid., 227, xxxiii.

matter of going in circles. The whirl was a very old element in Yeats' visual vocabulary, and there is a curious, reckless energy in the idea, almost cancelled in Part II of 'Nineteen Hundred and Nineteen', but always ready to reappear. In one short paragraph of the first version of *A Vision* Yeats uses the word 'whirling' four times: 'their whirling movement', 'a whirling for countless ages', 'all whirling perpetually' and 'this whirling'.[20]

So when he asks his rhetorical question about those who travel in the whirling dust he is paraphrasing the assertion that 'All men are dancers', but also doing something else. All men do quite a lot more than simply follow a gong, and to be 'in the Platonic Year' must mean to be caught up in something more than destiny or even cyclical time. The Platonic Year suggests renewal, as Helen Vendler remarked long ago, 'the possibility of perpetual genesis, of inexhaustible creation';[21] but it suggests even more strongly an order that can subsume all disorders, contain any amount of violence and turbulence without betraying their unruly, necessary energy.

III

In 1917, four days after their marriage, George Yeats 'surprised' her new husband 'by attempting automatic writing'.

What came in disjointed sentences, in almost illegible writing, was so exciting, sometimes so profound, that I persuaded her to give an hour

---

[20] *A Vision (1925)*, 121.

[21] Helen Vendler, *Yeats's Vision and the Later Plays* (Cambridge, Mass.: Harvard University Press, 1963), 96.

or two day after day to the unknown writer, and after some half-dozen such hours offered to spend what remained of life explaining and piecing together those scattered sentences.[22]

Fortunately the unknown writer didn't take Yeats up on this offer, and indeed replied to it in remarkably Yeatsian terms. 'We have come', he said, 'to give you metaphors for poetry.' Some eleven days later the couple began to keep a detailed record of their sessions—or at least the record begins after eleven days, it is possible that some earlier notes have been lost. The method of consultation shifted in late 1919 from automatic writing to a system of communication through a series of talking sleeps, or 'sleaps' as Yeats spelled them; and finally, by early 1921, settled into waking 'discussion'. The yield, George Mills Harper tells us, was 'more than 3600 pages in 450 sittings'.[23] *A Vision* was the literary and philosophical end product of all these visitations and inquiries. Yeats published an early version—too early, he came to think—in 1925 and another in 1938. The last recorded Automatic Script dates from 29 March 1920, although there are notebooks and a card file with later materials. All of this has been admirably edited by Harper and his team.

Accounts of this adventure tend to be coloured by one or both of two extreme tendencies. One is what seems to me an excessive worry about whether the spirits are real. The other is the habit of denigrating or even denying George's contribution to the brilliant, troubling, phantasmagoric contents of the sessions. Barbara L. Croft, for example, in an otherwise very sympathetic

---

[22] *A Vision* (1938), 8.   [23] *The Making of Yeats's A Vision*, vol. 1: x.

and well-argued book, thinks we need to wonder 'what portion of the material, if any', came from George's mind.[24] That 'if any' is extraordinary, however domineering we may feel Yeats' imagination to have been. Yeats himself addresses the question in a very subtle way in the second version of *A Vision*:

Much that has happened, much that has been said, suggests that the communicators are the personalities of a dream shared by my wife, by myself, occasionally by others—they have, as I must some day prove, spoken through others without change of knowledge or loss of power—a dream that can take objective form in sounds, hallucinations, in scents, in flashes of light, in movements of external objects.[25]

Yeats goes on to say he partly accepts and partly rejects this explanation, and what's interesting, of course, is that he accepts any part of it, since it clearly floats the implication that the whole adventure is *only* a dream, even if 'others' get into it. I think he is fudging the issue by associating what he calls the 'objective' sounds, scents, flashes, and movements with the methods of communication with the dead. Nothing more subjective, in my view, than a smell or a bit of poltergeist activity, whereas in our dreams a certain strange objectivity rules, since in them we seem to know things not available to our reasoning minds. The knowledge may be a delusion, and its delivery certainly doesn't require the intervention of spirits, but the most prosy of us will at times have been surprised by the esoteric authority of

[24] Barbara L. Croft, *Stylistic Arrangements* (Lewisburg: Bucknell University Press, 1987), 164.

[25] *A Vision (1938)*, 22–3.

our dreams, or even of certain distracted waking moments. If this material comes from our mind—and I don't doubt that it does—it comes from a mind we don't know. It's easy to imagine how exciting such an experience could become if pursued by two adepts of the Order of the Golden Dawn eager to let fiction do all the work it could. In the early 1950s George described the process as 'writing after suspending the will'; and in 1957 she said, in answer to a question about what she and Yeats saw themselves as doing, and what they imagined the spirit communicators were after, 'We thought they were expressing our best thought.'[26]

So that when Yeats speaks, in 'The Gift of Haroun Al-Raschid', his fictionalized account of the advent of the automatic writing, of 'truths without father', and of 'truths that no book | Of all the uncounted books that I have read, | Nor thought out of her mind or my mind begot', he may be protesting a little too much (and may know that he is doing so), but he is also describing a sense of discovery that could seem real enough to anyone.[27] The mind has mountains, to lift a phrase from Hopkins, even for people who have spent all their lives in the flatlands; and most of us would be dazzled if the mountains turned out to yield sacred texts rather than terrors or an empty, confused landscape.

[26] Quoted in Ann Saddlemyer, *Becoming George* (Oxford: Oxford University Press, 2002), 115, 132. In the first instance George Yeats may be remembering a phrase from *A Vision* regarding 'certain forgotten methods of meditation and chiefly how so to suspend the will that the mind became automatic, a possible vehicle for spiritual beings' (*A Vision (1925)*, liv).

[27] W. B. Yeats, *The Variorum Edition of the Poems*, ed. Peter Allt and Russell K. Alspach (New York: Macmillan, 1957), 467.

Not that the automatic script reads like a sacred text. I shan't describe it in detail—Harper's *The Making of Yeats's A Vision* has very well done what needs to be done in this respect—but a report of what an encounter with it feels like to a sympathetic but sceptical observer may help us to think about various engagements with chaos. The form of the script is essentially that of question and answer, although sometimes the questions are missing, and sometimes the spirits don't reply. There is literary criticism here, in the form of a long discussion of the possible meanings of Yeats' deeply autobiographical play *The Only Jealousy of Emer*; editorial consultation on the shaping of a later play, *Calvary*; an enormous amount of plugging away at the question of where to place whom on the chart of the phases of the moon (Keats at phase 14 or earlier, Blake at 16, Shelley at 17, and so on)—these sequences are mind-boggling for the sheer amount of time devoted to getting symbolic people into symbolic boxes. There is also a long and intensely crazy episode in which the Yeatses are in touch, through their 'instructors', with a seventeenth-century English aristocrat who wants them to bear her son, or give her son a second chance in a new incarnation. Fortunately, she was Yeats' mistress in one of his former lives, so this is not ghostly philandering, just a bit of *temps perdu*. At some point, I think, there is a suggestion that George too is related to the lady. All this comes to an end when Anne Yeats is born in February 1919—how could a mere girl redeem history and be the Messiah the Yeatses thought they were promised?

Harper compares the question and answer form to that of Socratic or Wildean dialogues, but the sessions often feel more like those parlour games in which you have to guess a name or a role by asking questions and getting yes and no answers. Daniel Dennett has a wonderful, anti-Cartesian account of how much 'revelation' you can gain this way, that is, how much a story-making mind can do with signals that are in themselves neutral.[28] Sometimes the questions or requests are distinctly loaded: 'Give Freudian analogies'.[29] Most of the time, though, the spirits—they multiply as the sessions go on, and include figures named Thomas of Dorlowicz, Rose, Leaf, Fish, Ameritus, Aymor—actually say something and here, I think, George deserves the credit for most of their finest lines. She's attuned to Yeats' thinking, of course, she's read his work, and she loves him; but she is not simply ventriloquizing what she thinks he wants to hear, and she doesn't say inordinately convenient things like 'We have come to bring you metaphors for poetry.' This line is reported (much later) by Yeats as an answer from the very first days of the experiment, before the extant record starts.

Here's a tiny selection of the answers the spirits offered through George—I've included the questions where they seemed necessary for the meaning.

Do not forget most of us are only forms under the reflection of real spirits

no use having a theory if it tires you

---

[28] Daniel Dennett, *Consciousness Explained* (New York: Little, Brown, 1991), 10–12.
[29] *Yeats's Vision Papers*, ed. Steve L. Adams, Barbara J. Frieling, and Sandra L. Sprayberry (Iowa City: Iowa University Press, 1992), vol. 1: 105.

In civilised man the innocence is so relative—I mean that it is not the
    innocence of the child but the innocence of lack of desire

a conception in sorrow gives sorrow to the child

What then do you mean by light?
Realisation of God

I am in no mood for lists

It is all outworn symbolism that you bring to bear on this

My head is full of a poem will that interfere?
No—medium more affected by stray irrelevances in the matter of
    writing afterwards

What is called astral light is really cosmic darkness

Was I passive enough just now
Not quite but you will improve

What is rythm and meatre
rhythm is the assimilation of the part by the whole
Metre is the mould of the whole without the parts

How does varience differ from conflict?
Variance produces forms of self knowledge of subjective nature—
    conflict only knowledge of objective good or evil

Can you give me your definition of the ugly?
Ugliness is the distortion produced by energy working on overindi-
    vidualised desire

Is reason a form of passion?
Of course

We never draw analogies

In what sense do you use the word Denial?
In all senses[30]

At times the spirits just hand over the subject matter to George, or she stops pretending, whichever you prefer. When the question is whether the medium is 'best fed or hungry', she doesn't hesitate or expand, she just says 'fed'. She also says at one point, 'Let medium take a hot bath then write'. She allows herself a little tartness too. Asked if Maud Gonne, the great elusive love of Yeats' life, will 'attain a wisdom older than the serpent', George says, 'She will attain to the wisdom of folly.'[31]

There are extraordinary *cris de coeur* as well.

Do not be tired—a point you perhaps do not realise is that script depends on the love of the medium for you ...

And in an obvious reference to the first days of their marriage, and George's perhaps deliberate and certainly desperate recourse to the automatic writing, she says:

The more you keep this medium emotionally and intellectually happy the more will script be possible now—at first it was better when she was emotionally unhappy but now the passivity is as small the opposite.[32]

---

[30] *Yeats's Vision Papers.*, vol. 1: 62, 64, 145, 83, 403, 447, 285, 289, 304, 321; vol. 2: 10, 24, 34, 46, 240, 465.

[31] *Yeats's Vision Papers*, vol. 1: 279; vol. 2: 270; vol. 1: 223.

[32] *Yeats's Vision Papers*, vol. 2: 323, 119.

Sometimes the questions and answers are simply, even ludicrously practical:

'You think we should go to Ireland just now?'
'Wise not to go for a long period of rest—yes'
'You mean not until after a long period?'
'Yes—better'.

The spirits can be solicitous: 'If you are not better in a week you had better see a doctor.' Sometimes they get a little fussy: 'If *I* give the time I like it kept.' And sometimes they are more relaxed: 'Take things as they come.' Asked (presumably) about an expected letter or parcel, one of them says 'I should advise going to big post office tomorrow morning to enquire.'[33] No harm in asking mere mortals about the mail. I think of G. Wilson Knight, the great Shakespeare scholar who was also a great believer in the spirit world, and whom I used to visit often in Exeter. He said once that he was rather concerned because the spirits had indicated a publication date for his book that differed from the one proposed by his publishers. I asked him what he was going to do. He said, 'I think I shall trust the publishers, because the spirits are often wrong.' There is an almost literal representation of this point of view in the Automatic Script. The spirit Ameritus comments 'you will say I am often wrong and that is so—for I only get men's thoughts.'[34] For Yeats, of course, even the wrong thoughts of dead men are precious, since they signify that no thoughts are lost. And there is something extraordinarily touch-

---

[33] *Yeats's Vision Papers*, vol. 1: 187, 80, 243; vol. 2: 23, 128.
[34] *Yeats's Vision Papers*, vol. 3: 24.

ing, I find, in this mixture of banality, high metaphysics and tormented psychology. The spirits are often wrong, but if they didn't exist they couldn't even be that.

IV

The speaker of Part III of 'Nineteen Hundred and Nineteen', unlike the wittily angry speaker of Part I and the hopelessly passive speaker of Part II, is a man trying to think calmly about human endeavour. He is lost because he can't escape the world he lives in and has no faith in anything that might be achieved in that world. He doesn't believe in spirits, right or wrong, and he represents, I believe, both Yeats' critique of his own system, and a level of depression he usually neither wanted nor thought he should give expression to. If the poem can't make use of Yeats' philosophy, it is not because it is temporarily out of reach or on another wavelength. It is because the poem, I want to suggest, is itself a mood of the philosophy, one of its very bad moments. The poem, until shortly before its end, when the figures in the whirling dust take us back to at least the possibility of other reaches of time, is asking what happens to the whole fabulous Yeatsian scheme if the gyres and phases and the Great Year are not merely questionable or a flimsy fabrication but *nothing*, mere camouflage for the sheer emptiness of all space and time outside our present life. 1919 would be the symbolic year that wasn't a year, a sort of temporal waste land, a zone that had fallen out of Platonic time and undone the notion of time in the process.

The sounds of the gong fade; the swan leaps into the desolate heaven. Or rather, the swan has leaped, disappeared into grammar as well as the unwelcoming sky—as the hero of Conrad's *Lord Jim* is at one point about to jump from the *Patna,* and then has jumped. 'She was going down', Jim says. And then, 'I had jumped ... It seems'.[35] Clearly the swan's leap is at the heart of the poem, and equally clearly the poem seeks both to register this deed and to ignore it.

When he writes of the 'moralist or mythological poet', Yeats probably has in mind some amalgam of Shelley and himself, and perhaps is glancing at Baudelaire and Mallarmé as well. The comparison of 'the solitary soul to a swan' is a little obvious and the poet's expression of satisfaction rather graceless; but perhaps this is just what Yeats means. The poem is flirting with prose. The image is satisfactory but not better than satisfactory. The speaker very quickly tells us what will more than satisfy him, and gives us an exact image, as if in 'a troubled mirror', of the swan he wants in the posture he wants:

> The wings half spread for flight,
> The breast thrust out in pride
> Whether to play, or to ride
> Those winds that clamour of approaching night.

Are playing and riding options facing the soul or different names for the same venture? The syntax is mildly ambiguous too. Is the soul ready to play those winds or ride those winds, or simply to play—or ride the winds? Any hesitation we may feel about what happens next must focus our attention on the moment of take-off, or just prior to take-off, that instant *just before* the event that appears so often in Yeats.

---

[35] Joseph Conrad, *Lord Jim* (Harmondsworth: Penguin, 1972), 88.

But now, curiously, Yeats seems to lose track of the swan for a whole tricky stanza—perhaps he is, in sense as in sound, imitating for us the man who is 'lost in the labyrinth that he has made'. In any event, the effect is truly startling, because when the swan returns, it has gone. It took off while the poem wasn't paying attention.

> The swan has leaped into the desolate heaven:
> That image can bring wildness, bring a rage
> To end all things, to end
> What my laborious life imagined, even
> The half-imagined, the half-written page;

The image that was satisfactory as long as the bird or the soul was poised for flight inspires rage when the creature has flown. Does it matter where the creature has gone? Of course. Who knows what will happen to it in that desolate heaven? It certainly won't be playing, and probably won't be riding the winds. And why is heaven so desolate, and only desolate? Where are the multitudinous inhabitants of the Great Year? But the poem also creates the nagging suspicion that other leaps were not likely to afford any great spiritual improvement—that a leap into worldly success, where the swan wins the Nobel Prize, for example, as Yeats did two years after he wrote this poem, wouldn't really alter things for the soul. The only thing that would really work, the poem seems to suggest, is being poised to leap but never leaping, because all leaps wreck the pure potentiality of the wings half spread for flight. This would be a little like believing that the only satisfactory way of dealing with spiritual revelation would be to pause at the moment of excitement before the message, and never listen to anything the spirits say.

This is also the suggestion, I think, of the strangely phrased 'even | The half-imagined, the half-written page'. The implication seems to be that a completely imagined or completely written page would go the way of all finished deeds, and good riddance to it. But the poet now, in his rage, is almost ready to get rid of the very idea of preparing to write, as if to cancel not only the swan's leap but also the previously treasured moment before the leap, the image of the soul in that instant before the brief gleam of its life is gone.

The argument is hard to follow here, in part because Yeats is miming his own confusion of mind, but it is not incoherent. Most of the arguing is done in the middle stanza, the one that takes place while the swan is leaping. A man makes a labyrinth in art or politics—no mention of the labyrinth a man might make in philosophy or with philosophy. He gets lost in it twice, it seems, once 'amid the labyrinth' itself and once 'in his own secret meditation' in the labyrinth. But he is not just lost. He is in another sense not lost enough, since he will leave his works behind him, he will be survived by all the bits of art or politics he has contrived, written and half-written, imagined and half-imagined, and so although he may manage to die, he can't actually 'cast off body and trade', there will be footprints and mess when he is gone, books or legislation everywhere, all of it, in the poet's current view, regrettable. At this moment the near repetition of the line about triumph marring solitude ('all triumph would | But break in upon his ghostly solitude'; 'For triumph can but mar our solitude') confirms a new thought. Not that success is crude and it is better not to have lived in the world of action, but that the world of action, of what we once pictured as success, is the domain of everything we got wrong. This is very hard to take, and the poet makes one last plea for the good intentions of the world that is no more:

> O but we dreamed to mend
> Whatever mischief seemed
> To afflict mankind,

The lurking rhyme of 'dreamed' and 'seemed' not only discreetly gives the game away, it reappears to finish off this last bid for a scrap of dignity for the old fantasies:

> but now
> That winds of winter blow
> Learn that we were crack-pated when we dreamed.

This is the last time we hear of dreams or mending in the poem, even false dreams or attempts at mending; although there is plenty of wind.

V

What's missing in this desolation is not Yeats' philosophy but any chance of philosophy. Or to put that another way, Yeats' philosophy is itself only a chance, a rescue of possibility, but it is as a chance that it matters. Even the firmest, most categorical of faiths cannot fill an empty heaven, and Yeats didn't have such a faith. But a cautious, precarious, even at times self-mocking belief in the persistence of life beyond death can turn desolation into something less than a certainty, and that may be all it needs to do.

'All Souls' Night', a poem written in 1920, and so towards the end of the period of close consultation of the spirits, appears both as an epilogue to *A Vision* and as the last poem in *The Tower*. It is full of the excitement of having 'a marvellous thing to say' but gives no indication of what that thing is. Its use of the word 'may' near the beginning is indicative of the poem's rather strange tone. 'A ghost may come'. The phrase suggests both possibility and permission. The ghost may come the way midnight has already come; or it may come the way the holder of a valid passport comes into a country.

> Midnight has come and the great Christ Church bell
> And many a lesser bell sound through the room;
> And it is All Souls' Night.
> And two long glasses brimmed with muscatel
> Bubble upon the table. A ghost may come;
> For it is a ghost's right,
> His element is so fine
> Being sharpened by his death,
> To drink from the wine-breath
> While our gross palates drink from the whole wine.[36]

A ghost may come. Or not. All that's really clear is that the time is appropriate; that the wine is there, untouched; that there is nothing to stop the ghost from showing up if it feels like it. We may wonder which two living people the glasses are for, and why they are not drinking. Perhaps they feel it's not respectful to offer the ghost the fumes from half a glass. Or perhaps there

---

[36] *Variorum Edition*, 470–1.

is only one person here, the speaker of the poem. One glass is for his 'gross palate', the other for whatever sequential shadows show up, the fumes of a full glass.

In any event, after this promising but slightly uncertain setting of the stage, the poet briskly moves away from his actual chances of a ghost audience, and tells us why he wants one. 'I need some mind that ... can stay wound in mind's pondering'. This wouldn't have to be a ghost's mind, although it seems the speaker will feel safer if it is. Why? Because he has

> ... a marvellous thing to say,
> A certain marvellous thing
> None but the living mock.[37]

None but the living mock. The phrase is strange, and shows more of Yeats' play with the possibilities of simple syntax. It feels like a displacement of something like 'the living will only mock'. But it doesn't say that; it doesn't even say that all the living will mock, or most of the living. It says only the living will mock; as if ghosts were not allowed laughter or scepticism, or as if they would never want to mock anything marvellous. And then the poet instantly, brilliantly corrects himself. The ghosts won't mock but it may help if they have exercised their right to breathe in a little muscatel, perhaps a lot of muscatel, since the thing the poet has to say is 'not for sober ear'. Slightly tipsy ghosts are a wonderful concept, and if the ghosts won't mock, or can't mock, they will, it seems, or they may—they *should,* the poem says—'laugh and weep an hour upon the clock'. The laughing and weeping

---

[37] Ibid., 471.

look towards the blessed and the damned who are named at the end of the poem, and the phrase itself is repeated there too, with the same rhyme of clock on mock. The suggestion, I take it, is that the marvellous thing is both good news and bad news, and that even a ghost might not know how to take it—that anyone, ghost, living human, even the poet himself, might legitimately be unsure whether to laugh or weep. And should therefore, as the poem says, laugh *and* weep, at least for a while.

Now follows a sequence of old friends, well, two old friends and an old enemy. Ghosts? Memories? Memories, it seems, of people sympathetic to the world of ghosts, or experienced in their contact with it, although each figure is summoned by the poet in language that applies just as well to remembering as to conjuring, perhaps tilting a little towards the latter as it goes on: 'Horton's the first I call'; 'On Florence Emery I call the next'; 'And I call up MacGregor from the grave'. All three of these persons were, in 1920, recently dead: Horton in 1919, Florence Farr Emery in 1917, MacGregor Mathers in 1918. Of the last figure Yeats handsomely claims that 'friendship never ends', even if Mathers was 'half a lunatic, half knave', and didn't react kindly when the poet told him so. But the poet turns out to be speaking only for himself, since he knows that Mathers, if he were to come back in any form except as a memory, would refuse to take even a sniff of the wine.

> But he'd object to the host,
> The glass because my glass.

'Friendship never ends' means something like 'I respect even the fellow's craziness and arrogance because they are his, and because he'll never change, whatever form of afterlife he has found'. Mathers is called not because he'll be supportive or attentive to the marvellous thing the poet has to tell, but because he knows and loves ghosts, and this is the kind of company the poet needs, at the cost of all other virtues.

> A ghost-lover he was
> And may have grown more arrogant being a ghost.[38]

And then the poet gives up, either because he could go on forever or because he knows no ghost is really going to appear. Or because the very idea of the ghost is finally only a metaphor for refinement of perception:

> What matter who it be,
> So that his element have grown so fine
> The fume of muscatel
> Can give his sharpened palate ecstasy
> No living man can drink from the whole wine.[39]

We have moved on from the initial fable of the ghost's right, and the division of pleasures: liquid for the gross palates of mortal humans, wine-breath for the ghosts. Now the ghost's scenting the wine produces an ecstasy unavailable to the living; and in context 'ecstasy' must mean something like *ivresse,* divine drunkenness. The living, we might say, can only get drunk. The ghost can get what the seeker of drunkenness was after. And now the poet repeats his lines about the sober ear, although with

---

[38] *Variorum Edition,* 473.   [39] Ibid. 473–4.

a different effect, as the movement of the poem has brought us to a different place. It's just 'the living' who mock now; not none but them. And we begin to understand what's wrong with having a sober ear, what a disability it is. It is rationality itself, a bar to all comprehension of everything except the obvious.

And yet. Yeats' marvellous thing, insofar as we know it from *A Vision* and a large number of his poems, is not an instance of the irrational. It has its own marvellous rationality. In his note on 'The Second Coming' he uses the word 'mathematical' four times in ten lines, and in *A Vision*, as we have seen, he likes to insist on the 'mathematical necessity' of his understanding of the world, on the 'exact mathematical proportion' of one movement of history to another. He thinks the supposed prophecies of Virgil may be linked to 'an apprehension of a mathematical world order', and he repeatedly cites or glances at 'recent mathematical research', meaning Einstein. The spirits communicating with him are working from 'a single geometrical conception'; and if Yeats finds their 'geometrical symbolism' difficult, it is because it is complex and elusive, not because it refuses the attentions of a sober mind.[40] Or is he saying perhaps that a truly sober mind will not be willing to offer such attention? The point perhaps, is not whether the system refuses sober thought but whether our sobriety will give it any consideration; whether a certain kind of rationality, let's say, has any time for other kinds.

Certainly Yeats' system is elegant in the mathematical sense— in the sense that mathematical proofs may be elegant.

---

[40] *A Vision (1925)*, lvii, 106, 125, 173; *A Vision (1938)*, 11, 80.

The whole system is founded upon the belief that the ultimate reality ... falls in human consciousness, as Nicholas of Cusa was the first to demonstrate, into a series of antinomies.

These antinomies are perfectly structured, always balanced, they trump all forms of confusion or disorder. 'All things are from antithesis'. 'Above all I imagine everywhere the opposites, no mere alternation'. Yeats, like Blake, believed in contraries but not in negation, and he distinguished carefully between life-creating conflict and logical error. 'I had never put the conflict in logical form, never thought with Hegel that the two ends of a see-saw are one another's negation, nor that the spring vegetables were refuted when over'. In his several repetitions of Heraclitus' phrase about 'dying each other's life, living each other's death', what finally seems appealing is not living after death (since dying after life is just as important) or even the interpenetration of all things, but the ideal, unending symmetry of the arrangement.[41] When in the poem 'Towards Break of Day' a man and a woman dream different dreams (of a waterfall, or a leaping stag), the dreams themselves are in dialogue in spite of their difference; they are not merely different.

> Was it the double of my dream
> The woman that by me lay
> Dreamed, or did we halve a dream
> Under the first cold gleam of day?[42]

[41] *A Vision (1938)*, 187; *A Vision (1925)*, 151, 176; *A Vision (1938)*, 72–3, 68, 197, 275.
[42] *Variorum Edition*, 398.

Only a believer in the deepest, most intricate forms of order could ask such a question.

We can't doubt the beauty or indeed the moral authority of such a scheme, and noting the elegant play of parallel and contrast in it, its splendid transcendence of the 'muddy, flooded, brutal self' and the realm of our 'broken toys', the very toys that 'Nineteen Hundred and Nineteen' reminds us we had when young, we can scarcely doubt its superior rationality.[43] But we can doubt its sustainability in any given, liveable world, and may be more inclined to do so the more rational and beautiful it is.

Yeats worries about this too, but he is not (mainly) protecting his scheme against rationalists, or hiding it from them;[44] and he is not only trying to obey the spirits who wish him to deliver their secrets very selectively or in disguise.[45] He is trying to recognize, to give a tone and shape to, his own scepticism while hanging on to his faith. And his faith can afford the fable of the tipsy ghost, the mildly garrulous evocations of old comrades,

---

[43] *A Vision (1938)*, 121, 147.

[44] He did talk about this. Helen Vendler quotes a letter in which he asks 'Will so-and-so think me a crazed fanatic?' *Yeats's Vision and the Later Plays*, 17.

[45] As one of them puts it, 'The information is not to be betrayed as to *source*—all else may be done.' Another says 'better not talk of it—it creates a centre of undesirable kind if in thought of many people'. And yet another, 'we are not pleased because you talk too freely of spirits and initiation ... because you speak to unbelievers you destroy our help'. Yeats is also told 'Remember warning—also personal secrecy always'; 'Do not talk psychics too much—you draw in strangers I do not like'; 'Script must be mentioned to no one and no one must be told you are sworn to secrecy'. *Yeats's Vision Papers*, vol. 1: 123, 176, 369, 378; vol. 2: 97, 133.

can even court the mockery the poet is seeking to avoid, the simultaneous laughing and weeping that come to seem indispensable, because it is a faith that has only two provisions or requirements: that the marvels remain possible, are not categorically denied; and that interpretations of the system are not confined to the literal, that figurative readings can also lead us to forms of truth.

Brenda Maddox shrewdly says Yeats preferred belief to disbelief, but we can go further. He hated disbelief, he thought it was immoral; and it may well be that his only real belief, the one he never joked about or swathed in fictions, was the belief in the permanent possibility of marvels, however often the hope of them was disappointed. There is also an element of kindness in such a view, and not only to himself. In a 1917 letter about psychical research Yeats wrote:

I think one should deal with a control on the working hypothesis that it is genuine. This does not mean that I feel any certainty on the point, but even if it is a secondary personality that should be the right treatment. The control believes that it is present for a purpose and is tortured by the feeling that it cannot carry out this purpose because we doubt its existence. As all experiments increase that torture by seeming part of our doubt, they should be given up so far as that control is concerned, until it has regained tranquillity. In fact the control should be treated as a doctor would treat a nervous patient.[46]

The repetition of the notion of 'torture' is important, as is the concept of treatment.

---

[46] Cited in *The Making of Yeats's A Vision*, vol. 1: 75.

In his early essay 'Magic' Yeats certainly speaks of specific claims in relation to marvels—that the borders of the mind and memory are shifting, that this larger mind and memory 'can be evoked by symbols'—but these are propositions most sceptics could endorse, and Yeats' emphasis finally falls on the 'quality of mind' that permits 'magic' to flourish.[47] A single page of the second version of *A Vision* is a key document in this respect. Yeats offers an admiring account of a great contemporary poem, makes himself more than usually clear about his beliefs regarding the afterlife, and takes a merciless and conclusive swipe at a famous philosopher.

The poem is Paul Valéry's 'Cimetière marin', the marine cemetery, or the graveyard by the sea, and you can see at once why Yeats likes it, or likes its opening movement—the atmosphere is not dissimilar to that of his own 'Byzantium'. As Yeats describes the initial action of the poem:

The sea breaks into the ephemeral foam of life; the monuments of the dead take sides as it were with the light and would with their inscriptions and their sculptured angels persuade the poet that he is the light ...

So far so good, even if the poet Valéry is not persuaded. But then Valéry takes a wrong turn.

After certain poignant stanzas and just when I am deeply moved he chills me ... and in a passage of great eloquence rejoices that human

---

[47] W. B. Yeats, *Essays and Introductions* (New York: Macmillan, 1968), 28.

life must pass. I was about to put his poem among my sacred books, but I cannot now, for I do not believe him.

One of the chief grounds for Valéry's failure to make the list of sacred books can be seen in the poem's most famous line: 'Le vent se lève! ... il faut tenter de vivre!' *Vivre*, that is, as opposed to making of sense of death, or dreaming of living on. By means of a curious pun on the word 'pass' Yeats takes Zeno's paradox, evoked in the poem, to suggest both that Achilles will not pass the tortoise and that time and life do not pass. But there is no doubt at all about what Yeats means. Valéry, like a proper rationalist (Yeats uses the terms 'metropolitan', 'reformer', and 'good manners', all pejorative in this context), has looked at a cemetery and has found only the dead there. His fault is not to have seen the cemetery as a place of ongoing life, or at least as a marker of a stage of ongoing life. Valéry, Yeats says in a very fine and revealing phrase, 'has learnt ... to deny what has no remedy'.[48] I take it Valéry is twice wrong, in Yeats' view: wrong to deny death rather than embrace it; and wrong to believe death, or indeed anything, has no remedy. And this is Yeats' own declaration of faith. It's not that he believes life does not pass, or does not believe in death. He believes that passing and death are part of a larger story; or that there could always be a larger story. He does not believe in disbelief, and is quite sure no one has any business rejoicing in it. He has no trouble with scepticism, and is himself a good deal more sceptical about the spirits than he is often thought to be—indeed than he often said he was. But the

---

[48] *A Vision (1938)*, 219.

step from scepticism to negative certainty he regards as a kind of crime.

This brings us to his note on the philosopher F. H. Bradley, at the foot of the same page. Here's the note in its entirety:

Professor Bradley believed also that he could stand by the deathbed of wife or mistress and not long for an immortality of body and soul. He found it difficult to reconcile personal immortality with his form of Absolute idealism, and besides he hated the common heart; an arrogant, sapless man.[49]

I should say that my own recurring reaction to this proposition is to want to side with Bradley. There is dignity in not pretending to console oneself when inconsolable, and you don't have to hate the common heart to be a stoic. Certainly I do not believe in the sort of immortality Yeats had in mind. But then each time I look at Yeats' actual phrasing I see again how very careful and generous it is. Do we believe we can stand by the deathbed of a loved one, *and not long for an immortality* ...? Surely this will depend on the nature of our love and our imminent loss, and our relation to love and loss and longing. And we can without question long for an immortality we do not believe in, even one we are sure we cannot have.

As for the escape from the literal, this is precisely what Yeats' famous and much misunderstood remark about 'stylistic arrangements of experience' insists upon. Responding to a doubt about 'the actual existence of [his] circuits of sun and

[49] *A Vision (1938)*, 219.

moon' Yeats answers that some are 'plainly symbolical'. But what about the others, the schemes involving historical eras?

To such a question I can but answer that if sometimes, overwhelmed by miracle as all men must be when in the midst of it, I have taken such periods literally, my reason has soon recovered; and now that the system stands out clearly in my imagination I regard them [the circuits of sun and moon] as stylistic arrangements of experience comparable to the cubes in the drawing of Wyndham Lewis and to the ovoids in the sculpture of Brancusi. They have helped me to hold in a single thought reality and justice.[50]

He is going farther than he needs to, meeting reason more than halfway. Every other page in *A Vision* suggests he regards his circuits as far more than stylistic arrangements. But the compounding of style, reality, justice, and thought is very impressive, and we need to realize that Yeats is showing us here the *least* he will claim for his system, not the most; and showing us that the least is a lot.

But what exactly is he saying? On one broad logical level the claim must be that if he simply, naively believed what the spirits told him while they were talking, he certainly knew better soon afterwards. In an earlier draft of the same passage he asked, 'Does the word belief, used as they will use it, belong to our age, can I think of the world as there and I standing here to judge it?' He means he is modern enough to know how problematic the concept of belief has become but wants to remind us that our age is not the only age there is—we can hear a nice little flicker of

---

[50] Ibid., 25.

combat in the phrase 'as they will use it'. At the end of this draft is a splendid first formulation of Yeats' concluding thought: 'he has best imagined reality who has best imagined justice.'[51]

Yeats may also seem to be saying, although he probably isn't, that if he once thought the spirits were literal entities he is now prepared to see them metaphorically. But his firmest assertion, as I understand it, is that although the spirits are real (the miracle is a miracle, that's not in question) they speak to us in metaphors, and that to take them literally, as one has to in the midst of miracle, is actually to misunderstand them. In a magnificent feat of what we might think of as muscatel logic, Yeats pretends to make a concession to reason while inviting reason to reach beyond itself, and especially beyond its bad habits of literalism. This then is what sober ears are: ears that hear only what they expect to hear; that hear nothing but the sound of their own sobriety; and whose owners have become arrogant without the excuse of being ghosts.

---

[51] Quoted in *The Making of Yeats's A Vision*, vol. 2: 410.

3

The Temptation of Form

'It might be argued that we now study the secret lives of words as if they were dreams'

FRANK KERMODE, *Romantic Image*

I

The imminent return of formalism is one of the great myths of contemporary literary study. It will save us from theory—if anyone is still interested in theory. It will save us from history—if history will offer us any kind of an opening. Formalism keeps producing wonderful critical books, for which anyone who cares about literature will be extremely grateful; but it never quite takes over, never gets to ride the promised wave.

There must be many reasons both for this recurring promise and this recurring failure to return in force, and the reasons may well include the possibility that in the Anglo-Saxon world at least formalism never *was* fully in force—they order these things differently in France, and Germany, and Spain and Latin America. But I want to suggest one mildly contentious reason, and I want to use this reason as a pointer to what I see as the necessary and attractive insufficiency of art at certain instants of its history or in certain encounters with the world. The reason is this. For all its considerable local critical interest, and for all its achievements of the finest attention and observation, formalism is not strong on argument or indeed on any kind of intellectual urgency. Even Roman Jakobson, for example, across the luminous detail of his descriptive work, is finally telling us that what he calls the 'supreme mastery' of Fernando Pessoa, say, is supreme mastery; and that Shakespeare's 'verbal art' is extremely verbal and extremely artistic.

There can't be anything wrong with an approach that produces such splendid results, and I have no quarrel with tautology as a method—it has the advantage of being (necessarily) true, which is no small thing. And we must recognize there are battles being fought, critical kingdoms at stake. Jakobson wanted to make sure we understood that a whole crew of critics and scholars was wrong to think of Shakespeare's Sonnet 129 ('Th' expence of spirit in a waste of shame') as logically disorganized, verbally impotent, or driven only by its rhyme-scheme, and he claimed that a proper formal (structural) analysis would put paid to 'such abusive, simplistic and impoverishing interpretations'.[1] Helen Vendler similarly, in her magnificent book *Our Secret Discipline*, asserts that critics have 'on the whole neglected Yeats's labour as

---

[1] Roman Jakobson. *Questions de poétique*, various translators (Paris: Editions du Seuil, 1973), 375.

a master of formidable techniques', and reminds us that 'Yeats's formal choices ... are not made at random'.[2] If these battles still need to be fought, if Shakespeare's art or Yeats' formal choices still need to be defended, or even noticed, then I know which side I'm on and I'm happy to join the fight, and to think of this book as part of the fight.

I'm not convinced, however, that these battlefields are where we want to linger, and one could accept all the achievements of the formalists, as well as their salutary tautologies, and seek to get somewhere else through the question of form. Vendler herself points the way in an earlier book, *Poets Thinking*. 'It is not obvious where "thinking" as such ... occurs in poetry', she writes, and yet her hope is 'to establish poets as people who are *always* thinking'. Always thinking and always showing us their thinking (rather than their paraphrasable thoughts), because poems are 'pictures of the human mind at work, recalling, evaluating, and structuring experience. The evolving discoveries of the poem ... can be grasped only by our participating in the process they unfold'.[3] Form is where we see the process, although of course it is 'useless', as Vendler comments, to attend to form without connecting it to content. 'Technique', she finely says, 'was never, for Yeats, without conceptual meaning'—a meaning itself always in movement.[4]

---

[2] Helen Vendler, *Our Secret Discipline* (Cambridge, Mass.: Harvard University Press, 2006), 2, 87.

[3] Helen Vendler, *Poets Thinking* (Cambridge, Mass.: Harvard University Press, 2004), 2, 9, 119.

[4] *Our Secret Discipline*, 5, 153.

Angela Leighton makes a similar case for form as process, and manages the astonishing feat of getting the slippery multiple meanings of the word to work for it rather than against it. Form 'is an abstraction from matter' (as in a Platonic form) which 'is also subtly inflected towards matter' (as in physical form). Sometimes it escapes from the body, sometimes it needs a body, sometimes it is a body. It is 'hollow, ghostly', Leighton says in a wonderful reading of a passage from Coleridge, 'and therefore morphologically greedy for substance'. 'Form', she adds a little later, 'is not a fixed shape to be seen, but the shape of a choice to be made.' Of its role in Yeats' work in particular Leighton says 'form is simply the rhythm of what came and went, and was saved in the various forms of language itself'.[5] There is a flicker of tautology in the sentence but it enlarges the meaning rather than loses it, and the practice has an illustrious antecedent in a famous claim made by T. S. Eliot about the relation of Joyce's *Ulysses* to the genre of the novel, where the word 'form' racks up three meanings in a single sentence.[6]

No modern critic or theorist of poetry is likely to accept without reservations Pope's argument that 'the sound must seem an echo to the sense', because of the clear separation of the two

[5] Angela Leighton, *On Form* (Oxford: Oxford University Press, 2007), 1, 8, 16, 169.

[6] T. S. Eliot, '*Ulysses*, Order and Myth', in *Selected Prose*, ed. Frank Kermode (New York: Harcourt, Brace, Jovanovich, 1975), 177: 'If it is not a novel, that is simply because the novel is a form which will no longer serve; it is because the novel, instead of being a form, was simply the expression of an age which had not sufficiently lost all form to feel the need of something stricter.'

elements, and the clear subordination of one to the other—although Pope's word 'seem' perhaps lets a little modern haze in through the neo-classical back door.[7] We are more likely to be told that the sound *is* the sense, because form *is* content, or at least that, as Cleanth Brooks says, 'form and content cannot be separated'.[8] But the fact that the two elements live together doesn't mean they can't be talked about separately, and they are conceptually quite different. It is for this reason that their inextricability at any given moment is so interesting. Derek Attridge puts this very well when he says

Our habit of skimming for sense ... doesn't stand us in good stead when it comes to poetry, which simply cannot work *as* poetry if it is read in this way. This is not because poetry is only or primarily sound, but because it is *in* sound—and above all sound in movement—that its meanings are produced and performed. To remember a poem is ... to remember words spoken in a certain order.[9]

Still, modern critics discussing such matters often get closer to Pope than we (or perhaps even they) might imagine. Attridge himself, in another book, writes of the 'aptness' of the metrical form Yeats chooses for his poem' 'Easter 1916'. It 'contributes to the unease that hovers about even the apparently ordinary

---

[7] Alexander Pope, 'An Essay on Criticism'. In *Poems* (New Haven: Yale University Press, 1963), 155.

[8] See Susan Wolfson, *Formal Charges* (Stanford, Calif.: Stanford University Press, 1997), 6 for this quotation, and *passim* for an excellent discussion of this question.

[9] Derek Attridge, *Poetic Rhythm* (Cambridge: Cambridge University Press, 1995), 2–3.

descriptions in the opening of the poem', and it 'enacts the transformation which is [the poem's] subject: the quotidian becomes the remarkable, the casual becomes the compulsive'.[10] There is an interesting play here between the ideas of aptness and unease, which points precisely to a certain edginess in the formal activity I am pursuing.

What Helen Vendler predominantly finds in Yeats' formal achievement is a satisfying mimesis of content. 'As we follow a Yeatsian stanza through its unfolding, we often come to admire the way in which unusual or irregular stanza-rhythms and thought-rhythms seem effortlessly to agree'. The 'heavy vowels' of the last section of 'The Tower' 'seem like the dull sounds of clods of earth falling into a grave'. In 'Meru', a long sentence about hermits in the snow 'mimics their prolonged exposure to the elements'. Vendler says she 'would argue' that a certain section of 'Meditations in Time of Civil War' 'could not have seemed aesthetically credible to Yeats ... unless its *thematic* notions found a mimetic reflection in the structure of the stanzas narrating them'.[11] I take it she would also argue, indeed is arguing, that *nothing* could seem aesthetically credible to Yeats if some such consonance were not present.

Now this consonance can contain considerable amounts of noise and disorder. There is nothing timid or reductive about Vendler's readings. She too writes of 'unease' ('rhythmic unease

---

[10] Derek Attridge, *The Rhythms of English Poetry* (London: Longman, 1982), 327, 328.

[11] *Our Secret Discipline*, 297, 195, 201, 362, 241, 180, 269 [some quotations deleted].

The stanza's 'syntax strains against its rhymes, its rhymes against its rhythms', Vendler says.[53] And we can add: its rhythms slip in and out of emphasis, so that the very idea of rhythm becomes a question, a negotiation between absence and riches. As Jahan Ramazani very finely says of the last stanza of this part of the poem, 'The poet's rage would assimilate him to the destructive force of the winter wind, erasing his words and his world ... The transcendental impulse ... is ... a rage not only against formal order but also against the self and language.'[54] And yet this rage itself finds words, and courts and simulates disorder rather than succumbing to it. What it succumbs to is the limitation of being a poem. If prose is the ruin of verse, as Agamben says, then Yeats is only lending his words to ruin before taking them back again.

But then he gets even closer to ruin. How do we read these words, the opening of the last part of the poem?

> Violence upon the roads: violence of horses ...

The easiest scansion perhaps is to reverse the iambic beat a couple of times:

> Víolence upón the róads: víolence of hórses ...

This way the line settles down twice, but only three of the five beats are actually iambs. We could imagine, at a stretch, an entirely regular scansion:

---

[53] *Our Secret Discipline*, 70.

[54] Jahan Ramazani, *Yeats and the Poetry of Death* (New Haven: Yale University Press, 1990), 125.

> Violénce upón the róads: violénce of hórses …

But this is somehow more disturbing than the already unsettling music of the previous scansion. We're working too hard, and the word violence seems to be a source of trouble in its own right.

About this part of the poem Frank Kermode says 'the modulation occurs as the wind drops, metrical change becomes an element in the plot, the rhythmical plot'.[55] The matter couldn't be better put, and all I'm doing is chasing this insight—and trying to say what the plot is.

> But now wind drops, dust settles; thereupon …

Well, thereupon, there are five more lines and the poem ends with the strange rhythms of:

> Bronzed péacock féathers, réd cómbs of her cócks.

My friend and colleague Susan Stewart says 'it's hard to make any of these words unstressed'. There is something bumpy happening in the middle of the line, some sense of trouble in the lady's offering, an awkwardness that doesn't appear to have anything to do with witchcraft, which in its way often goes very smoothly.

The crucial line, though, is the one I've already quoted, and that begins the poem's last sentence; reveals the plot, or what there is to be seen of it. There is a regular iambic line hiding here, like a ghost or a well-behaved child.

---

[55] Frank Kermode, 'The Anglo-Irish Hyphen', in *The Hopkins Review* 1.1 (Winter 2008).

> But nów wind dróps, dust séttles; théreupón ...

But almost anyone is going to read the line as if it starts iambic ('But nów'—couldn't be better) and indeed ends iambic, but in the middle gives us two spondees in a row, therefore five stressed syllables one after another:

> But nów wínd dróps, dúst séttles; théreupón ...

It's hard to exaggerate the ominous effect of this rhythm, especially in conjunction with what the line is saying. This is the calm after the whirlwind (after thunder and tumult and evil gathering head), the end of the violence upon horses and the vision of the daughters of Herodias, and for a moment we breathe more easily. But only if we are not listening. If we are listening we hear the drumbeat of a different nightmare, and we know some sort of second coming is at hand, in this case the reappearance of the man Yeats describes as 'an evil spirit much run after in Kilkenny at the start of the fourteenth century'.[56]

The grammar does an interesting trick as we read of 'that insolent fiend Robert Artisson'. The reasonable question is, Who on earth is that? But we don't ask it. For a moment we think we know the fellow. That Robert Artisson. We can't remember anything about him but surely that lurch, those eyes, that hair are familiar. The same goes for Lady Kyteler. Didn't we always know she was associated with him in some way? And we certainly know what those peacock feathers and cocks' combs were all about: that old black magic. The effect fades, of course; but it also

---

[56] *Variorum Edition*, 433.

lingers. There is a touch of the same familiarity in Yeats' saying Artisson was 'much run after in Kilkenny'. Not: the demon who terrified the Irish countryside but some sort of playboy of the spirit world, the blonde beast whom all the girls fancied. When we do a little digging and find out more about this couple, the results are also interesting, but different. Now we really are in a world of stereotypical sorcery. Alice Kyteler was condemned as a witch in 1324. She had four husbands, is said to have poisoned the first three and robbed a fourth of his senses by 'philtres and incantations'. She and her friends left dismembered animals at crossroads for 'a spirit of low rank, named the son of Art', who appeared in various forms, as a cat, a hairy black dog, and a Negro.[57] Black magic indeed. Artisson was said to be the source of Lady Kyteler's wealth, so he was not just a pretty face. But this intriguing lore adds up to something less than our old imagined intimacy. We knew them better before we knew them.

VIII

The metre and rhythm of the poem, we now see (or hear) turn out to work in some of the same ways the rhymes and line divisions do. They reinforce meanings available otherwise, and they complicate and unsettle those meanings. They also do something else. They organize the music of the poem, and they gesture to what is not music in it, to whatever there is in the poem that escapes music. They tell a story of their own, parallel to the visible plot of the poem,

[57] A. N. Jeffares, *A New Commentary on the Poems of W. B. Yeats* (Stanford: Stanford University Press, 1984), 235.

but not quite the same. The move is from ironic grace to a flirtation with prose, and from there to a smart and rhythmic rage. It would be a very good poem without its last part, but it would be all about anger and failure and it would not exceed its own bounds. It would express failure but it would not incur failure's expense, to borrow Blackmur's phrase. For Part VI is not only obscurely and enduringly troubling in its own right, it alters everything that went before. The metrical uncertainties of Parts II and III, for example, become forms of impatience, and their reward is a displaced and bungled doom. When we hear, whether we are attending to them or not, the five stressed syllables of 'now wind drops, dust settles', and work our way through that linked chain of strong, occluding consonants (w/w, d/d/d, st/st), we are pulled out of anger into difficulty and suspense. We don't know what we are waiting for, and we don't know how to wait for it. And even when we see the fiend and the love-lorn lady, and hear the emphatic stresses of the last line, we are still waiting perhaps, because we may feel they are not it, whatever it is. Like the Magi, we are unsatisfied by the turbulence on offer, and alone with our scarcely identifiable appetite.

Auden was almost right to say, in his elegy for Yeats, the poetry makes nothing happen.[58] This is because a poem is itself something that happens. A poem is an action, and as Hannah Arendt says in another context, 'it is the function ... of all action, as distinguished from mere behaviour, to interrupt what otherwise would have proceeded automatically and therefore predictably'.[59] Of course many provisos and restrictions leap to mind. If

[58] W. H. Auden, *Collected Poems* (London: Faber and Faber, 1991), 248.
[59] Hannah Arendt, *On Violence* (New York: Harcourt Brace, 1970), 30–1.

a poem isn't any good, nothing will happen. Even if a poem is a masterpiece, nothing will happen if we don't allow it to. And most important of all, it is characteristic of this sort of happening that we find it very hard to say what has happened—that is why it sometimes seems as if nothing has happened.

We are already some way beyond the simplest claims of formalism: that mastery is mastery and art is art. Good poems tells us a lot about the world and about ourselves—or rather they tell us things and they show us things, and they play those things out on our nerves through their formal resources. The formal resources are aids to expression, and are themselves modes of meaning, as I hope the preceding analysis has suggested.

Michael Ragussis, in what is still perhaps the best single essay on the poem, suggests that the end of the work is 'the exact opposite' of an apocalypse. 'The poet is not exalted through vision. He escapes nothing except falsehood.'[60] This is where admirers of the last part of the poem can meet up with its detractors. There is no vision. But not, I would say, because we witness the exact opposite of an apocalypse. Rather we witness—or go some way towards experiencing—what Yeats has found instead of an apocalypse, or a weasels' apocalypse, if you like. Form and content come together in a brilliantly failed, spectacularly impoverished act of the imagination. I don't mean Yeats represents failure, I mean he has brought himself to the limits of success. This is not the dead imagination of Beckett, with its weird afterlife. In Yeats the imagination is still as alive as it ever was, only

[60] Michael Ragussis, *The Subterfuge of Art* (Baltimore: The Johns Hopkins University Press, 1978), 102.

at the end of its tether. It has to make do with the images it can find; and it has just enough strength to see what it can't see, to glimpse how thoroughly the images it has discovered are not the real thing, are not the revealed iconography of an actual, disastrous apocalypse. Here again, as so often, Yeats makes us think of the strategies of Gothic fiction; shows us a monstrous face to keep us from thinking of the further, faceless monstrosities we are really afraid of.

In 'Nineteen Hundred and Nineteen' the poet uses form to point beyond form, to give us a glimpse of the 'formless darkness' he evokes in another poem in *The Tower*. 'The finally exemplary moments' in Yeats, Seamus Heaney remarks, 'are those when this powerful artistic control is vulnerable to the pain and pathos of life'.[61] And even more than vulnerable, at times, I am suggesting: insufficient. At such points Yeats simultaneously gestures towards order and abandons the gesture. 'A little formalism turns one away from history', Roland Barthes once said, 'but a lot brings one back to it'[62]—and history, in this context, would be precisely the world that the poem, any poem, might light up with its own strange news.

---

[61] *Finders Keepers*, 115.

[62] Roland Barthes, *Mythologies*, trans. Annette Lavers (New York: Hill and Wang, 1994), 112.

4

The Old Country

'For were it not the part of a desperate physician to wish his diseased patient dead, rather than to employ the best endeavours of his skill for his recovery'

EDMUND SPENSER, *A View of the Present State of Ireland*

'The Irish propensity for violence is well known; at least to the English'

CHARLES TOWNSHEND, *Political Violence in Ireland*

I

'My mission', Gladstone famously declared in 1867, 'is to pacify Ireland.'[1] He can't have thought the task was going to be easy but neither, perhaps, can he have fully registered the intricate contradictions lurking in the very idea. They lurk there both because of what pacification turns out to mean and because the

[1] Quoted in Charles Townshend, *Ireland: The 20th Century* (London: Arnold, 1999), 6.

word Ireland signifies so many things, and is so full of restless mythologies. Of course the names of all nations are full of mythologies, but some are fuller than others and the mythologies are different. For a people 'dispossessed by event', as Eavan Boland suggests, 'an extra burden falls on the very idea of a nation'. And certainly there are persons of quite opposed political stripes who regard the idea of a pacified Ireland as at best an oxymoron. An Ireland at peace, or in Boland's words 'resolved and healed of its wounds', would in any case be something else.[2]

Until very recently my impression was that pacification did not, in the nineteenth century and after, to borrow a phrase from Yeats, have the sinister connotations it acquired in the later twentieth century, when it was used so cynically by American strategists in Vietnam, and when napalm was one of the chief instruments in the bringing of peace to enemy villages—an operation memorably shown in Francis Ford Coppola's film *Apocalypse Now*. But the *Oxford English Dictionary* offers an interestingly ambiguous first definition:

To bring (a country, people, etc.) to a state of peace. Also: to impose peace upon; to subdue.

And among earlier uses the *Dictionary* gives us Gibbon's 'When he had subdued or pacified the Barbarians of the Danube, Constantius proceeded by slow marches into the East.' Subdued or pacified, take your pick. Did Constantius subdue some Barbarians and pacify others or is there only one operation in play? It

[2] Eavan Boland, *Object Lessons* (New York and London: Norton, 1995), 128–9.

does seem as if there is trouble lurking in the term itself, almost as if it were one of Freud's antithetical words. Peace exists perhaps, but no one can be 'brought to' it without violence. If they could, they wouldn't need pacifying in the first place.

There are contradictions to be found even in the most brutal simplifications of the notional 'Irish question'—the simplifications themselves carry, like a fever, the contradictions they seek to hide. For many long years Ireland was for English politicians both an insoluble problem and not really a problem, merely a sort of eternal nuisance. It would never go away; you could always get it to go away, at least for a while. Something of this mode of thinking—its curious, unacknowledged doubleness—has coloured many Irish minds too, especially when the North considers the South and the South considers the North. What's intractable is unmistakable; and also often oddly missing from the discussion.

I'm going to concentrate here on certain aspects of Ireland as a figure—as a supposed locus of violence and contradiction—in certain poems: in 'Nineteen Hundred and Nineteen', of course, but also in Andrew Marvell's 'Horatian Ode' and another poem by Yeats; in two poems by Paul Muldoon, from one of which I have borrowed the title of this chapter; and much more briefly, in works by Seamus Heaney, Tom Paulin, and Eavan Boland. I have already suggested, following Helen Vendler, that poems allow us to see poets thinking, and here I'm trying to watch them thinking about this doubleness itself. My continuing suggestion is that on this subject no one ever says only one thing at once. For the poems this is an advantage. Since I am far from wanting to endorse any sort of automatic association of Ireland with violence, I must be as clear as I can about my topics here: namely, the effect of repression in Marvell; of lawlessness in Yeats; and of a constant, muted or fully voiced threat in the four other poets.

II

Marvell has already been associated with Yeats in just this context. Michael Bell says the 'Horatian Ode' is the 'nearest English counterpart' to Yeats' 'Easter 1916' among 'meditations on the necessity of political violence,'[3] and David Bromwich makes the same association, saying rather slyly that Marvell's Ode is 'the work of a poet who needed, like Yeats, to appear much farther above the battle than he actually was.'[4] I think the connection of Marvell's poem to 'Nineteen Hundred and Nineteen' is even stronger than it is to the earlier Yeats work, since both poems—the Ode and 'Nineteen Hundred and Nineteen'—were written during or just after a time of war in Ireland, and a brief glance at what many critics regard as one of literature's greatest exercises in equivocation will help us, I suggest, to see something of what poets usefully can do in violent times. There is an intriguing historical pile-up in the fact that Hannah Arendt, in her book on violence, takes two lines from Marvell's poem—'How fit he is to sway | That can so well obey'—as an 'old adage', although she does refer to a book on Marvell, if not to Marvell's Ode.[5] It is an old adage. Marvell's

[3] Michael Bell, *Literature, Modernism and Myth* (Cambridge: Cambridge University Press, 1997), 50.

[4] David Bromwich, *Skeptical Music* (Chicago and London: Chicago University Press, 2001), 9

[5] Hannah Arendt, *On Violence* (New York: Harcourt Brace, 1970), 39.

most recent editor, Nigel Smith, calls it 'a well-known sententia', and refers us to Plato's *Laws*.[6] But Plato's wording is rather different ('No one will ever make a commendable master without having been a servant first'), and Arendt is quoting as an adage a very particular formation of an idea with many turns.

The full title of the poem is 'An Horatian Ode upon Cromwell's Return from Ireland'. It was written in June or July 1650. Cromwell had come back to England in May of that year, after what another editor calls a 'devastating war in Ireland',[7] and when Fairfax, who was at that point commander-in-chief of the English army, refused to march on Scotland without the provocation of an invasion, Cromwell took over the job, and set out for Scotland in late July. The poem, Smith says, 'must have been composed in this brief interlude between Cromwell's two celtic forays'.[8]

Marvell, like Yeats, insists on the word 'now'. 'The forward youth', the poem opens, 'that would appear | Must now forsake his muses dear.' ''Tis time to leave the books in dust | And oil the unusèd armour's rust.' This is why 'restless Cromwell could not cease | In the inglorious arts of peace', and 'burning through the air he went' to blast the head of Caesar, alias Charles I.[9]

> 'Tis madness to resist or blame
> The force of angry heaven's flame:

---

[6] Andrew Marvell, *The Poems*, ed. Nigel Smith (London: Pearson and Longman, 2003), 277.

[7] Andrew Marvell, *Complete Poetry*, ed. George deF. Lord (London: J. M. Dent, 1984), 55.

[8] *The Poems*, 267.   [9] Ibid. 273–4.

> And, if we would speak true,
> Much to the man is due,
> Who from his private gardens ...
> Could by industrious valour climb
> To ruin the great work of time.[10]

Towards the end of the poem Marvell portrays the invasion of Scotland as a liberation, and makes an ethnic joke of questionable taste. The Pict, it seems, has a 'parti-coloured mind'—a mind that is partisan and coloured in various shades, but he is also likely to try to hide behind his kilt, or literally 'shrink underneath the plaid'—the traditional costume of his incoherence. The poem closes with another joke, but this time darker, and unmistakably aimed at Cromwell—even Cromwell's supporters would have to see the warning, and the irony, here.

> And for the last effect
> Still keep thy sword erect:
> Besides the force it has to fright
> The spirits of the shady night
> The same arts that did gain
> A power, must it maintain.[11]

The trope is a form of understatement, or understatement by reversal. Besides the magical powers superstition attributes to the shape of the cross, you are going to need a quite literal weapon to hang on to your power. This proposition is elegant and witty; graceful because it dresses a tough thought in indirection. But the metaphor hiding in the trope is eerier. In order

---

[10] Ibid. 274–5.   [11] *The Poems*, 279.

to stave off spirits with a sword, you will have to hold it upside down, for hard military work against flesh and blood opponents you will need the other end. And then you will need to flip it back again if the spirits of the shady night should happen to return. This is manageable but comically awkward, and suggests a political unreadiness when you ought to be most ready. Still, the half-playful note remains until we register Marvell's deepest and most interesting implication: the spirits might really, practically be more trouble than your worldly enemies, and it won't actually matter how you hold your sword then, since neither superstition nor force will help you. And how could a world of regicide not have its ghosts? Scholars point us to Homer and Virgil here, but the eeriness mounts higher then. In Homer Odysseus certainly manages to keep the ghosts of the underworld away with his sword, but Aeneas, although told by the Sibyl to keep his blade unsheathed, finds himself, as Smith reminds us, waving it at unearthly creatures who can't be touched by it, *frustra ferro diverberet umbras*.[12] Not too much power over the spirits here, as Marvell must know all too well.

The poem appears to many critics to be riddled with ironies; to others those critics themselves are riddled with anachronistic modernist suspicion, incapable of believing a man might mean what he says. In the heyday of the New Criticism in America— or even before, in 1947 to be precise—Cleanth Brooks argued for the unresolved ambiguity of the work and said 'the final appeal in this matter ... is not to what Marvell the Englishman must have thought, or even to what Marvell the author must

[12] *The Poems*, 279.

have intended, but rather to the full context of the poem itself'.[13] Douglas Bush, in 1952, affected not to understand what Brooks meant by these distinctions, 'since the poem did not get itself written by some agency outside of Marvell' and he insisted that all the ironies are the invention of a 'good modern liberal' who doesn't like the tough politics of the seventeenth century.[14]

Is Marvell a Royalist pretending to be a Cromwellian, a recovering Royalist who has become a Cromwellian, or is he seeking a position above the fray, an intricate balance of opposing views? He is almost certainly seeking a position in the literal sense, that is, trying to get a job in Cromwell's new dispensation; but he seems to be going about it in a rather strange way. There are lines that are openly sympathetic to Charles:

> He nothing common did or mean
> Upon that memorable scene:
> But with his keener eye
> The axe's edge did try.

Still, there's no reason why the king's behaviour on the scaffold couldn't be admired by someone who had come to think his politics were reprehensible. But then what about the poem's talk of 'ancient rights', and the 'helpless right' that in his dignified dying Charles does not invoke? He did nothing common

> Nor called the gods with vulgar spite
> To vindicate his helpless right,

---

[13] Cleanth Brooks, 'Marvell's *Horatian Ode*', in John Carey (ed.), *Andrew Marvell* (Harmondsworth: Penguin, 1969), 193.

[14] Douglas Bush, 'Marvell's *Horatian Ode*', ibid. 207, 200, 203.

> But bowed his comely head,
> Down, as upon a bed.

The great work of time is ruined, and power, it seems, speaks louder than justice:

> Though injustice against fate complain,
> And plead the ancient rights in vain:
> But those do hold or break
> As men are strong or weak.[15]

There are real difficulties here, but the riddle of rights and power can be unravelled, if we follow Marvell's argument very closely, ideally supplementing our efforts by a reading of *Leviathan*. The king has rights, but a 'helpless right' is compromised in its legitimacy as well as materially defeated. The state has rights too, and a duty to protect the lives of its citizens, who are interested, as Hobbbes says, in 'their own preservation' and a relief from that unruly war of all against all which is the natural condition of humans without government. To say that 'ancient rights … hold or break as men are strong or weak' is not necessarily to preach *Realpolitik,* since as Hobbes also says, 'Covenants, without the sword, are but Words, and of no strength to secure a man at all.'[16] A right's claims to moral respect, that is its existence as a right rather than a brute fact of power, depends on its chances of remaining unbroken. Well, perhaps this is *Realpolitik* as long as these chances depend on the sword, but

---

[15] *The Poems,* 276, 275.
[16] Thomas Hobbes, *Leviathan* (London: Penguin, 1985), 223.

it is a line of thought with a long pedigree, and the argument is clear enough.

I don't believe the same can be said for the following lines, which seem to me the real test case of what the poem is up to:

> And now the Irish are ashamed
> To see themselves in one year tamed:
> So much one man can do,
> That does both act and know.
> They can affirm his praises best,
> And have, though overcome, confessed
> How good he is, how just,
> And fit for highest trust.

Two lines later we get Arendt's old adage:

> How fit he is to sway
> That can so well obey.[17]

It is very difficult to read these lines as anything other than ironic, as the words of a poet pretending to say what propaganda no doubt really did say. Annabel Patterson offers an interesting refinement of this idea when she suggests that Marvell's 'strategy is to shift responsibility for evaluating the Irish campaign to the conquered Irish, thereby putting to lively use the "praise even by enemies", and hopefully avoiding any question of the massacres of Wexford and Drogheda'.[18] Marvell would not be pretending

---

[17] *The Poems*, 277.
[18] Annabel Patterson, *Marvell and the Civic Crown* (Princeton: Princeton University Press, 1978), 64.

to say what he says, he would be saying it, but in a mode that left room for disavowal. He wouldn't have to be ironic, though—evasive or cautious would do—and this Marvell would have side-stepped the question that comes up again and again in the criticism. David Loewenstein hears 'a grim irony' in the lines—Brooks also writes of 'grim irony'—but no sort of judgement on Cromwell.[19] Milton thought the Irish campaign had been conducted 'in full accordance with the will of God'[20]—the enemies were Catholics, after all—and Marvell, in this view, thought the same. Harold Toliver agrees we are likely 'to expect irony' in the lines, 'since Cromwell's hand had been unusually heavy at Wexford and elsewhere', but thinks Marvell simply accepts the brutality of war for what it is. 'For the lines cannot be taken ironically without totally inverting the eulogy'. Toliver goes on to quote:

> So much one man can do,
> That does both act and know …
> How good he is, how just,
> And for highest trust.[21]

Toliver is right that the eulogy, if it is one, can't be taken ironically; but his ellipsis is revealing. Even as he tells us the irony is not there he takes away the lines that make it look as if it is.

Brooks and Bush actually converge in their opinions at this point, since their disagreement is about the attitude to be

---

[19] David Loewenstein, *Representing Revolution in Milton and his Contemporaries* (Cambridge: Cambridge University Press, 2001), 199.

[20] Ibid.

[21] Harold Toliver, *Marvell's Ironic Vision* (New Haven and London: Yale University Press, 1965), 190.

imputed to Marvell, not about the plausibility of the proposition as it stands. Brooks says 'the Irish are quite proper authorities on Cromwell's trustworthiness ... for they have come to know him as the completely dedicated instrument of that state whose devotion to the purpose in hand is unrelenting and unswerving'.[22] He thinks this is ironic but not simply sarcastic. Bush, continuing his campaign against unnecessary complication, says there is no need for anyone to go 'twisting Marvell's plain words into irony'; but then adds that 'in regard to what seems to us a strange assertion, we must say that he is indulging in some wishful thinking'.[23]

Whether Marvell is ironic or wishful, evasive, grimly supportive, or plainly pragmatic, the same gap opens up between the proposition and what feels like its opposite. Or to put that more strongly, between the proposition and any likely form of the truth. We are asked to believe, or at least consider the possibility, that the Irish have not only been pacified, or tamed, as Marvell puts it, picking up a word the English have been using about the Irish at least since Spenser, but that they are full of admiration for their supposed pacifier. This is, to put it mildly, not the way the story of Cromwell plays in any area of the Irish imagination I have heard of, and when Thomas Davis, for instance, writes of 'Cromwell's cruel blow', there aren't any intimations of 'how good he is, how just' anywhere in the vicinity.[24]

---

[22] 'Marvell's *Horatian Ode*', 193

[23] Ibid., 208.

[24] W. B. Yeats (ed.), *A Book of Irish Verse* (London and New York: Routledge, 2002), 90.

Of course, Marvell's poem is addressed to the English, but even so the sheer improbability of the claim won't go away, and I find it hard to believe Marvell didn't know exactly what he was doing in this respect. He wanted the unlikelihood, the gap is everything, rhetorically and morally. The claim would still be improbable even if it were true, and the gap opens rather than closes the space for rival interpretations. Those of us who find it hard not to hear reservations in Marvell's voice—echoes, let's say, of the massacres he is not mentioning—need to recognize that the strongest possible support of Cromwell's actions is not incompatible with remembering who the man's enemies are. A hyperbolic, even fanciful representation of their submission could well perform something of the oblique and intricate task carried out by the semi-playful warnings at the end of the poem. This would also be the sense of Loewenstein's (but not Brooks') 'grim irony': the irony would be in Cromwell's situation not in Marvell's tone, and the elaborate untruth would underline it.

English readers, at least, could latch on to the drift of the hyperbole, which is also the literary method of Marvell's poem on Cromwell's first anniversary as Lord Protector—if anyone ever could receive this improbable tribute, it would be Cromwell. And once it moves on from its precarious claim about the Irish the poem is no longer chiefly about justice or truth or even about power. It gives us an idealized portrait of a ruler, of the very idea of rule, of the state of what Walter Benjamin calls 'legal violence'. Cromwell not only holds 'the highest trust', he is 'fit' for it. Not only does he sway us but he is 'fit ... to sway'. In these dream regions even the Irish might be swayed rather than sullen. I'm pretty sure it is anachronistic to hear overtones of coercion in Marvell's use of the word 'confessed', but then if no Irish person has been forced into this unlikely testimony the English fantasy stands out all the more clearly.

Of course it wouldn't feel like a fantasy for anyone who believed it, or even anyone who very much wanted to believe it, and in this respect Marvell's poem, like Yeats' 'Nineteen Hundred and Nineteen', turns out to concern not a set of facts but a mentality; a mentality, what's more, that depends on words making gestures towards a reality they will never be able to tie down. Independently of whatever reading we reach of his own attitude, Marvell is offering us a reminder of how dangerously words can dangle away from meaning; just as Yeats reminds us how furiously they can bite their own tail.

III

The curse of Cromwell, in Yeats' poem of that title, is not a simple one. 'Cromwell's house and Cromwell's murderous crew', the long consequences of Cromwell's attention to Ireland, are all there is to be seen 'far and wide'.

> The lovers and the dancers are beaten into the clay,
> And the tall men and the swordsmen and the horsemen where are
>   they?

The poem's desperate answer, both abject and assertive, is that Irish servitude is even more ancient than English conquest:

> There is a beggar wandering in his pride
> His fathers served their fathers before Christ was crucified.[25]

---

[25] W. B. Yeats, *The Variorum Edition of the Poems*, ed. Peter Allt and Russell K. Alspach (New York: Macmillan, 1957), 580.

The next stanzas—there are three more—blame Cromwell's curse for the dominance of commerce and competition ('money's rant is on | He that's mounting up must on his neighbour mount'), assert the ghostly reality of the culture Cromwell killed, and finally picture the poet as the friendless inhabitant of 'an old ruin'. He does however possess two forms of knowledge unavailable to Cromwell's men or their descendants, and perhaps not all that available to the vanished Irish gentry. He knows 'the time to die'; and he knows 'that things both can and cannot be'. He doesn't strictly—this is what the poem suggests rather than says—know the time to die. He knows there is such a time, but he will also, like the rest of us, seek a deferment when the time comes—indeed we might read this poem as precisely the granting of this deferment.

The other knowledge, though, is very real, and prolongs the ambiguity of Marvell's poem, even as it changes the disposition of the actors. The story still concerns a beleaguered mentality, but the siege is over, and history has spoken. What 'can and cannot be' in 'The Curse of Cromwell' is the continuing life of the lost culture, 'the swordsmen and the ladies' who 'can still keep company ... though all are underground'. Can keep company and pay for a poet and for a fiddler to entertain them. 'This brilliantly colloquial poem', as Roy Foster calls it,[26] is a ballad, its speaker is a popular rhymer, almost a folk-singer, not the Modernist poet. It begins with

[26] Roy Foster, *The Arch-Poet* (Oxford: Oxford University Press, 2003), 576.

a relaxed address to an ongoing community ('You ask what I have found'), even if the poet at the end seems to have only 'dogs and horses' to talk to, and the refrain at least mimes a mode of resignation:

> O what of that, O what of that
> What is there left to say?[27]

We have heard that rhetorical question, or its very close relative, in 'Nineteen Hundred and Nineteen'. In this case asking four times if there is anything left to say certainly keeps the ball in the air, and the ballad's recurring rhythms prepare us for the recall of old habits and the return of the dead.

The poet casts himself as a 'servant', like the beggar 'in his pride', and delights in a vision of the past where his employers were his 'friends':

> I came on a great house in the middle of the night
> Its open lighted doorway and its windows all alight,
> And all my friends were there and made me welcome too.[28]

He is recording a dream, a haunting, but in a poem as in a movie, what's shown can't simply be unshown. It can be corrected, but there is a sense in which such corrections never completely take—the uncorrected image persists in the record. There is no doubt that the poet wakes, and wakes into what another poem calls the desolation of reality. 'But I woke in an old ruin that the winds howled through.' There is no doubt that the dead are dead, or that Cromwell's curse is still drastically

---

[27] *Variorum Edition*, 580, 581.   [28] Ibid. 581.

in operation. But the house lights up in the mind and in the poem, as if it were the kinder truth that history chose to hide, whether in 1650 or 1919, and that current reality has very little chance of finding. It is just as important that such things can be as that they also cannot. Writing to Dorothy Wellesley about this poem, and stretching its implications beyond Ireland, Yeats said Cromwell was 'the Lennin of his day'.[29] The spelling is Yeats' own.

IV

Part IV of 'Nineteen Hundred and Nineteen' reads, in full:

> We, who seven years ago
> Talked of honour and of truth,
> Shriek with pleasure if we show
> The weasel's twist, the weasel's tooth.

This is pretty conclusive. What more is there to say, or left to say? Everything that has been aired so far in the poem is fiercely summarized here. All excuses are abandoned, the swan has flown, there are only weasels left. The shrieking of our pleasure is particularly nasty, both the sound and the idea. I don't believe the poem ever leaves the weasels' world from this point on, although that world is finally visited by ghosts, heathen goddesses and the creatures of a creepy, sleazy mock-apocalypse. But there is more to say, even apart from the description of

---

[29] *The Arch-Poet*, 576.

these visitations, and Yeats says it in the crucial fifth part of the poem.

It looks like a straightforward affair, picking up on the tone of Part IV—even though there doesn't seem to be anything to pick up on by way of content. Everyone notices that the repeated 'Come let us' seems to announce the world of the folk song, or the hymn. If you look up 'Come let us' in the English Poetry Database, you will find 399 entries, from Ben Jonson's 'Come, let us here enjoy the shade' to Charles and John Wesley's 'Come, let us with our Lord arise', but the invitation is always to do something rather calmer or kinder than mocking, and 'Come let us mock' is not among those 399 entries. The Database goes only from 600 to 1900, but still, 1400 years of absence is not nothing. There is a further oddity in the verse, a form that Helen Vendler calls 'very peculiar'. It seems to behave like a folk quatrain, except that it has a fifth line. And the beat, instead of the more usual 4-4-4-4 or 4-3-4-3, is 3-4-3-4 with an added 3-beat line. So that the last line, producing an effect of neatness through the rhyme, produces an effect of oddness through seeming short. Each time the fifth line continues the thought without any logical difficulty, and each time it seems scarcely necessary. As if there is nothing more to say and Yeats is saying it.

But there are intricate insinuations in the thought itself, which seems at first very simple: let us mock everyone, including the mockers. The great are to be mocked, it appears, because they tried so hard, because they 'had such burdens on the mind | And toiled so hard and late' and failed to achieve anything. They are perhaps to be mocked also for wanting to leave 'some monument behind', a memorial to themselves rather than anything useful, but the real sting is in the apparently extra last line of the stanza. They had so much on their minds that they didn't think. They are exactly the people who form the 'we' in Part I of the poem. Greatness is a kind of absorption in fantasy. It's not that they didn't worry enough about the wind of random violence, or the consequences of the fact that the worst rogues and rascals have not died out, or that they defied these conditions. They didn't even think of them.

The wise are treated a little more kindly. They 'fixed old aching eyes' on their calendars and tried to look into the future. But they couldn't even see the present, and they are left to 'gape at the sun', blinded presumably but not possessed of any insight, no closer to wisdom than wise people, in this view, ever are. But their failure, the tone and diction here suggest, was to be expected. They couldn't let us down because we were never going to turn to them. Still, their irrelevance, the irrelevance of wisdom, is an important feature of the world of the weasels— and of the world that gave birth to the world of the weasels.

The good are the ones who come in for the most complicated mockery, and we learn a little more about these people. They are not just good but they have, we learn at the turn of the line, 'fancied goodness might be gay'. These must be Nietzscheans of the nicer sort, people who want to practise *le gai savoir, die fröhliche Wissenschaft,* without ruthlessness. But there is more. They have also fancied that goodness might be 'sick of solitude', and in this frame of mind or body 'might proclaim a holiday'. A holiday from goodness? A holiday of goodness? The suggestion, I think, is that this is what gaiety is: goodness on holiday. But the thought that goodness could want a holiday only because it was sick of solitude ruins the whole proposition. We scarcely need the mockers Yeats is invoking to see what's wrong here. With heroes like these, who needs enemies? It's striking too that these figures are sick of precisely what is offered elsewhere in the poem as some sort of comfort: 'ghostly solitude'. The shriek of the wind seems especially angry, no doubt because this is a story where an engaging but perhaps impractical thought (that goodness might be gay) turns unto some sort of pathology, the social programme of the sick and lonely crowd.

And the mockers? Many readers have wanted to interpret the mockery of mockers as a form of double negative making a positive, a reaching for a perspective beyond mockery, but I can't see it. The invitation here—no, the instruction, there is no 'Come let us' any more—is simply not to let the mockers escape, precisely to cancel the possibility of a further moral perspective. There is nothing to do but mock, and that is what we are going to do. Both the verse and the logic get a little lame here—'maybe' seems a feeble line ending, and why would the mockers lift a hand to help if they are already busy mocking?—as if to show that even mockery is running out of energy, but there is, once again, a fierce kick in the last line:

> for we
> Traffic in mockery.

We don't just mock, we're in the mockery business, and the word 'traffic' takes us back to the last stanza of Part I, with its unobtrusive shift from elegiac vanishing to literal vandalism to the black market.

'That country round', we read there,

> None dared admit, if such a thought were his,
> Incendiary or bigot could be found
> To burn that stump on the Acropolis,
> Or break in bits the famous ivories
> Or traffic in the grasshoppers or bees?

This is already weasel territory since every line introduces a new logical reservation, and the first line introduces two. If anyone thought, not of burning the stump but that there might be someone who would, they would not admit to having that thought; and the thought itself, we learn, concerns not only the 'ancient image made of olive wood', which is how the stump was earlier and more politely described, but also the delicate carved ivories of Phidias, and the 'golden grasshoppers and bees' used as ornaments or decorations, apparently, in ancient Athens. And not only do we encounter the thought that people may or may not have, and won't admit to if they have it, but it now seems as if burning and bigotry are not the only threats, since trafficking in the ornaments is also a possibility. For good measure the printings of this poem up to and including the one in *The Tower* all have a question mark at the end of this grammatically quite unquestioning sentence.

What have we learned through this excursion into mockery that we didn't know at the end of Part IV, when we saw the weasel's twist, the weasel's tooth? We know who the weasels are not, and we know that the discredited great, wise, and good no longer rule the world. But we also know something else, which the sharp finality of Part IV hid from us, and which the garrulous quality of Part V reveals. These are not just any old weasels, they are betrayed weasels, they are still angry at the great, wise, and good precisely because they once believed in them, or in some of them. Right after the haunting evocation in Part I of the mother murdered at her own door by a drunken soldiery, we learn that random violence has not newly arisen in the world, but has come back, creating horror in direct proportion to our belief that we had got rid of it. Yeats' first title for this poem was 'The Things Return' or 'The Things that come again'.

> The night can sweat with terror as before
> We pieced our thoughts into philosophy,
> And planned to bring the world under a rule,
> Who are but weasels fighting in a hole.

In his drafts for 'Nineteen Hundred and Nineteen' Yeats is very clear about the myth he has in mind, the dream that occupied the space between 'before' and 'now'. The poetry isn't so good but the lineaments of the idea stand out well. There is 'a general confidence in future days', there is 'a speedy remedy for obvious wrong'.

> And we would say...
> That all men soon would be both fed and learned.

And all this even though 'we still had empires and such things'.

The great point about this mentality, I have suggested, the great historical and mythological point, is the shock, even the violence of its sudden death. Its rosiest claims can't ever have been true, and it can't ever have been quite as false as its deceived believers were to come to think. What is true is that those believers couldn't get over the bad news—no, couldn't get past the moment when they learned the bad news. That's why the weasels are so given to mockery, and are not going to stop, however tired they get.

What all this adds up to—it is worth adding it up very carefully—is a mixture of anger and disappointment so rich and complex that we have to wonder what else has gone into it, and indeed whether anger and disappointment are, as they seem to be, the main ingredients. There is a famous but not fully articulated clue to the mentality in the title of George Dangerfield's *The Strange Death of Liberal England*, first published in 1935. Strange in this context must mean startling or surprising, unexpected, quite unlooked for. Except that, it turns out, every single cause of this death was solidly, unsurprisingly in place before it happened. Dangerfield says in his Foreword that he had planned to tell the story of 'the approaching catastrophe of which the actors themselves were unaware'. Very dramatic. 'But it wouldn't have been true'. The truth is that the catastrophe was not the Great War but what was happening before the war. 'The War hastened everything—in politics, in economics, in behaviour—but it started nothing.'[30]

Paul Johnson, in a Preface to a 1966 reprint of the book is even more emphatic. 'Liberalism had entered a period of slow decline'—nothing strange about that. 'Liberal England'—the England of 'Free Trade, classical scholarship, strict religious observance, public probity and reformist zeal' in Johnson's rather partial formulation—'was not killed; it died a natural, if unpleasant death.'[31]

[30] George Dangerfield, *The Strange Death of Liberal England* (London: MacGibbon and Kee, 1966), 13–14.

[31] *The Strange Death of Liberal England*, 9, 12.

Strange means strange and not strange at all. But we may also find lingering here, in both Dangerfield's and Johnson's tone, a third tier of implication: people do continue to find strangeness in what's not strange. How strange of them. The very thought takes us back to the sentences I have already quoted from Henry James about the outbreak of the First World War, where the now ruined faith appears to concern not only Liberal England, but a liberal world. Or perhaps we should speak not of faith but of illusion, a strange belief that a strange death was not in the offing. Here again is what James wrote on 5 August 1914 to Howard Sturgis:

The plunge of civilization into this abyss of blood and darkness ... so gives away the whole long age during which we have supposed the world to be, with whatever abatement, gradually bettering, that to have to take it now for what the treacherous years were all the while really making for and meaning is too tragic for any words.[32]

Five days later, on 10 August, he wrote to Rhoda Broughton:

You and I, the ornaments of our generation, should have been spared this wreck of our belief that through the long years we had seen civilization grow and the worst become impossible. The tide that bore us along was then all the while moving to *this* as its grand Niagara—yet what a blessing we didn't know it. It seems to me to undo everything, everything that was ours, in the most horrible retroactive way.[33]

[32] Quoted in F. W. Dupee, *Henry James* (New York: Delta, 1965), 248–9.
[33] Henry James, *Letters, Volume IV* (Cambridge, Mass: Harvard University Press, 1984), 713.

And six months later, on 5 January 1915, he wrote to Betham
Edwards:

I find it difficult to give verisimilitude to a world for which this
huge bloody trap was all the while set and which childishly didn't
know it.[34]

The key phrase in each letter, surely, is 'all the while'. Here
the strangeness is not in the belief that the Great War did or
did not put an end to a whole culture, but in the fact that the
culture had been doing itself in for some time. This is Dangerfield's thesis, but with a deep and terrible extension. Dangerfield sees Liberalism failing even in, especially in its last
apparent victories. James sees the Victorian and Edwardian
eras—his 'long age'—as a kind of ghastly fraud or confidence
trick. A whole apparatus of improvement was secretly preparing the ground for butchery, blood and darkness. Of course
there are differences within James' phrasing. There's a very
large gap between childish ignorance and blessed ignorance
and a larger one still between blessed ignorance and tragic
ignorance. Especially when the tragedy may lie in a condition
of mind that is not really ignorance at all. That's what I take the
words 'give away' and 'treacherous' as proposing in the earliest
of the three letters, although in a mode of reluctance, of simultaneous disclosure and concealment. We knew what the years
were all the while making for and meaning, even as we told
ourselves a quite different story. In such a reading the phrase

[34] Quoted in Lyndall Gordon, *A Private Life of Henry James* (New York
and London: W. W. Norton, 1998), 361.

'have to take it' has a horrible resonance. The grammatical referent of 'it' is 'the world' that was supposed to be bettering, and isn't—or rather never was. But 'have to take it' suggests both passive suffering, as if we were not to blame, and deep complicity in the error, as if indeed blame were just what we have to take.

James' language, his mixed mode of apparent explicitness and lurking reluctance, allows us to understand the three tiers of Dangerfield's strangeness a little better, and take one further step. The death of Liberal England, or more grandly, the end of all hope for a bettering world, is signalled, even caused by the war that came out of the blue. No, none of this came out of the blue, neither the death nor the end nor the war, it was all in preparation all the time, there to see if anyone cared to see. What is strange is that anyone thought it strange, and that many continue to think it strange, to inhabit their own amazement as if it were the only place to be. But of course the logic of all this knowing and not knowing also suggests a drive or an anxiety of a different order. We need the strange, we need to be startled by what we couldn't afford to expect. Between our blessed ignorance and our tragic pretence of ignorance lies the whole indispensable narrative of surprise.

I thought until recently that the rage and the wit in 'Nineteen Hundred and Nineteen' have mainly to do with the colossal error the poet is attributing to himself and his generation. The error was not to want the world to get better but to believe that it would get better because we wanted it to. This error is certainly an important part of the picture, but what the showy army and the sleepy horses and the all too awake dragons finally suggest, what we pick up in all the poem's oblique, apparently ornamental verbal activity, is not only illusion but the active creation of a whole culture of denial. In James' thought there is plenty of folly, and some degree of complicity in an illusion that was just too welcome. But there are no weasels. In Yeats there are weasels who managed to persuade themselves that their own nature had died out. Until one day—we return to the story of the grand break, the great event, the strange death—the whole flashy picture fell apart, law, public opinion, fine thought, philosophy, world-rule, picturesque parades, parliament and king and all. But then all this also means that even weasels can have unweaselish dreams, and perhaps they were not entirely wrong to try to forget their nature. Or not all of them were wrong. The degree of Yeats' disappointment suggests that the old hopes were something more than empty folly.

In his essay 'Thoughts After Lambeth', written in 1931, and so some time after the assertions in James' letters and Yeats' poem and only four years away from Dangerfield's 1935 book, T. S. Eliot offered what may be the deepest and most insidious reading of the mentality we are looking at. His ostensible subject was his dislike of the term and concept 'generation'. The complaint is interesting, but it's the tail-end of the remark that matters most in the present context.

When I wrote a poem called 'The Waste Land' some of the more approving critics said that I had expressed the 'disillusionment of a generation', which is nonsense. I may have expressed for them their own illusion of being disillusioned, but that did not form part of my intention.[35]

The illusion of being disillusioned is an extraordinary idea. Eliot is affecting not to believe in either disillusionment or the concept of a generation and he is telling us he can't have written about any such things. But he is willing to imagine he may have expressed something that was no part of his intention, and he is willing to guess at what that something may be. It can't be disillusionment because he doesn't believe in that, and it can't be ordinary illusion because his contemporaries are so sure they are disillusioned. What's left is their subjectively perceived disillusionment, which Eliot knows to be an illusion. We can ask how Eliot knows this, and we can wonder whether a person who thinks himself or herself disillusioned just isn't disillusioned. What else is required but the thought? Stendhal was fond of writing of people who 'thought themselves unhappy', and we could ask the same questions of him. How do people really feel if they only think themselves unhappy? What is the actual content of a mind caught up in the illusion of disillusionment? We note that Eliot doesn't say the affectation or posture of being disillusioned, which might make more historical sense. These people genuinely believe in their own thoughts, that's how illusions work. They say, 'Now we see what the treacherous years were all the while making

[35] T. S. Eliot, *Selected Essays* (New York: Harcourt, Brace and World, 1964), 324.

for'; they say, 'All right, we are but weasels fighting in a hole'. And these emphatic and final declarations of disillusionment are statements of illusion because ... I'm not quite sure how to finish this sentence. But I take the implied claim to be this. Disillusionment is an illusion, not because Eliot or we think it is, but because it can't overcome the intricate reluctance that shadows its fierce frankness. It knows only that it doesn't like the treachery of the treacherous years. It knows nothing of the detail of the deceit, it hasn't even started to understand its own history. Even the weasels know that there is more to history than name-calling, and that their thinking even for a moment that they weren't weasels is itself an important historical phenomenon. But all they can do, even now and ever after, is call themselves weasels.

V

This, I think, is where the unmasked but still kicking delusion in Yeats' poem meets up with the gap between proposition and probable truth in Marvell's 'Horatian Ode'. In both cases—and in many other literary cases too, of course—a claim and its counterclaim dominate the page, in Yeats because 'we' can't get over the death of our hopes, and in Marvell because the poem holds up a manifest fiction in front of us and asks us what we are going to do about it. In both cases the writing covers and uncovers an unsettling thought or memory, and can do this because it cares, for different reasons, about what is covered and what is uncovered. The writing is not ambiguous but it is double, and double in the way that only poems and novels and plays are, or can be when they want to be. Many of the arts deal in the difference between truth and error—the arts of politics and lying, for example—but neither politicians nor liars can be interested in the ongoing quarrel between truth and error, or between two truths, or two errors. And there is another kind of artist, the one identified by the philosopher Harry Frankfurt in his little book on bullshit, who doesn't deal in truth and error at all because he doesn't care about the difference. This is the reason why Frankfurt thinks bullshitting is worse than lying. The liar at least cares enough about the truth not to tell it. We might even think there is a science in all this, in Hobbes' sense: 'that conditional knowledge, or knowledge of the consequence of words, which is commonly called science'.[36] It is among the consequences of words, or perhaps one of the conditions for the very existence of words, that they can tell us the truth, that they can lie to us, that they can be used to scramble or bury the difference between truth and lies, and that they can do whatever they are doing in the poems we have been looking at. And before trying to say a little more closely what that is, and what it has to do with violence, I want to look at another poem.

The poem I have in mind is from *Horse Latitudes*, a recent volume by Paul Muldoon, and it is called 'The Old Country'. The poem is about Ireland—well, about Ireland and several other places, some of them in the mind; in our minds. Here's how the poem begins. The title continues into the first two lines,

[36] *Leviathan*, 131.

although even then the sentence remains verbless. The form is the Petrarchan sonnet.

The Old Country

Where every town was a tidy town
and every garden a hanging garden.
A half could be had for half a crown.
Every major artery would harden

since every meal was a square meal.
Every clothesline showed a line of undies
yet no house was in dishabille.
Every Sunday took a month of Sundays

till everyone got it off by heart
every start was a bad start
since all conclusions were foregone.

Every wood had its twist of woodbine.
Every cliff had its herd of swine.
Every runnel was a Rubicon.[37]

The old country looks at first like a focus of nostalgia for a poorer but less complicated life—those clotheslines and gardens and cheap half-pints of beer—but there are already hints of something else in the bad start and the foregone conclusions, to say nothing of the conversion of every runnel into a Rubicon. In fact the poem very quickly settles into the suggestion that no noun can appear in public unless accompanied by its all too

[37] Paul Muldoon, *Horse Latitudes* (New York: Farrar, Straus and Giroux, 2006), 38.

predictable adjective, that this is a world where clichés grow and thrive with a kind of Pavlovian associative regularity. Say start and you'll get a bad start; say conclusion and it will be foregone. There are some very funny variants on this mode—'the shouting but for which it was all over', and the elaborate

> Every time was time in the nick
> just as every nick was a nick in time.[38]

The artery in the above quotation runs into two sorts of traffic: on the roads and towards the heart. But mainly, all the way through the poem, there are lots of straight versions of the declarative, inescapable sentence:

> Every resort was a last resort
>
> every lookout was a poor lookout
>
> Every hope was a forlorn hope
>
> Every slope was a slippery slope
> where every shave was a close shave
> and money was money for old rope
> where every grave was a watery grave
>
> Every escape was a narrow escape
>
> Every pig was a pig in a poke
>
> Every malt was a single malt
> Every pillar was a pillar of salt
> Every point was a point of no return

---

[38] Ibid. 41.

> Every track was an inside track
>
> Every flash was a flash in the pan
>
> Every fervour was a religious fervour
>
> Every pit was a bottomless pit[39]

Listing the sentences in this way—and there are more—emphasizes the monotony of the syntax, which is an important part of the effect. But the variations matter too. Here's another complete section:

> Every runnel was a Rubicon
> where every ditch was a last ditch
> Every man was 'a grand wee mon'
> whose every pitch was another sales pitch
>
> now every boat was a burned boat.
> Every cap was a cap in hand.
> Every coat a trailed coat.
> Every band a gallant band
>
> across the broken bridge
> and broken ridge after broken ridge
> where you couldn't beat a stick with a big stick.
>
> Every straight road was a straight up speed trap
> Every decision was a snap
> Every cut was a cut to the quick.[40]

[39] Paul Muldoon, *Horse Latitudes* (New York: Farrar, Straus and Giroux, 2006), 39, 41, 43, 44, 45.

[40] Ibid. 40.

And here's how the poem ends, returning to where it started:

> But every boy was still 'one of the boys'
> and every girl 'ye girl ye'
>
> for whom every dance was a last dance
> and every chance a last chance
> and every letdown a terrible letdown
>
> from the days when every list was a laundry list
> in that old country where, we reminisced,
> every town was a tidy town.[41]

The intricate form of the poem—thirteen linked sonnets, with four lines appearing four times and five lines appearing twice, and with the line about the tidy town opening and closing the poem— contributes strongly to its particular, haunting effect. The work is funny, it is sharp, it says something about nostalgia and about the uses of language; and finally it becomes completely claustrophobic, feels endless because it's circular. The fun becomes a kind of prison and the old country, apparently a place one can't return to, becomes a place one can't get out of. There are innocent or positive clichés— the single malt, the gallant band, the snap decision—but the balance is overwhelmingly melancholy: last resort, poor lookout, slippery slope, no return, bottomless pit, last ditch, burned boat, cut to the quick, last dance, last chance, terrible letdown. It's a sad old country, but these metaphors and moans are not the worst thing about it. The two worst things about it are that it has nothing except clichés to think with or talk with, and that it speaks only in these airless, exceptionless sentences. It would be bad enough if most resorts

---

[41] Ibid. 46.

were last resorts, and if most lookouts were poor. But for every one to be this way amounts to a kind of negative perfection, where everything lives up to a Platonic dream of its own worst self. The best one can hope for is to shift from a damaging stereotype to a harmless one, but there doesn't seem to be a chance of anything other than stereotype.

The poem remains funny because it's a picture of how we think when we are scarcely thinking at all, and if we're laughing it may mean that we not only recognize this mode of memory but that we have already got out of the old country. This is how we talk about the place now, all we have left are largely negative idealizations. That's what an old country is, or one version of what an old country is: the past frozen in such a way that we can't really get at it. But then perhaps we stop laughing, and perhaps we haven't left. And when Muldoon points us towards Yeats' 'Nineteen Hundred and Nineteen' by way of a quotation from its harshest lines we may wonder how far we have got from that world where only violent revelations have any real authority, where only violence can defeat denial. 'Every cut was a cut to the quick', Muldoon writes,

> when the weasel's twist meets the weasel's tooth
> and Christ was somewhat impolitic
> in branding as 'weasels fighting in a hole', forsooth,
>
> the petrol smugglers back on the old sod...[42]

The assimilation of Christ, presumably in the frame of mind in which he drove out the moneylenders from the temple—the

---

[42] *Horse Latitudes*, 40.

incident is mentioned later in the poem—to the furious voice in Yeats' poem berating a whole generation for believing the world was getting better and could be brought 'under a rule' suggests that even Christ doesn't know how far the world has fallen from virtue. 'The thing to have done', the poem says later, with a calm acceptance of everything still bothering Christ and Yeats, 'was take up the slack'. 'Every track was an inside track', the poem says with knowledgeable satisfaction, not a note of complaint. And best of all, 'every platitude was a familiar platitude'. Much better than your strange platitudes any day.

I'm not suggesting there is any call for violence in the Muldoon poem, rather the reverse, but I am interested in the way it moves so smoothly back into Yeats' time and preoccupations, and the way it pictures a world in which language parts company with reality and even takes its place. The grammar and voice of the poem cheerfully deny that there is a need for anything other than the next ready-made sentence—it will see us through to where we need to be. And yet the poem as a whole, without a single murmur of critical comment, converts this denial into a parade, a picture of a whole country skating on thin linguistic ice.

A slightly earlier poem by Muldoon, from the volume *Moy Sand and Gravel*, gives us a similar sense of the old country, and here the violence is more perceptible, although it still appears only in a name and glance (and a game and a pun and a political situation). The poem is called 'Tell', and starts off with an evocation of a boy who has taken to playing out the story of William Tell and his son, rather than the imaginary battles with American Indians that used to occupy his time.

> He opens the scullery door, and a sudden rush
> of wind, as raw as raw,
> brushes past him as he himself will brush
> past sacks of straw
>
> that stood in earlier for Crow
> or Comanche tepees hung with scalps
> but tonight must past muster, row upon row,
> for the foothills of the Alps.[43]

In a shed near the house 'almost a score' of men are peeling apples 'for a few spare | shillings', and talking to each other. As the boy opens the door of the shed one of them 'mutters something about "bloodshed" | and the "peelers"'. He may be speaking of the group, the apple-peelers, and the boy may think this—perhaps the pun is meant to divide him from the men, and from us. But he is far more likely to be speaking of policemen. Either way there is a frozen moment, and all that happens in the poem now is that the boy's father winks at him. The extraordinary last sentence of the work occupies two and a half stanzas. All the men have put their knives down.

> All but his father, who somehow connives
> to close one eye as if taking aim
>
> or holding back a tear
> and shoots him a glance

---

[43] Paul Muldoon, *Moy Sand and Gravel* (New York: Farrar, Straus and Giroux, 2002), 19.

> he might take, as it whizzes past his ear,
> for another Crow, or Comanche, lance
>
> hurled through the Tilley-lit
> gloom of the peeling-shed,
> were he not to hear what must be an apple split
> above his head.[44]

We can imagine a whole variety of contexts for this scene: a recent death, a reaction to it, a plan for violent action, a concern about informers, perhaps an accusation against a particular informer, or a scheme for punishing that person. What's important is that the father both 'tells' and doesn't tell his son about all this—he 'tells' him among other things that one shouldn't tell tales—and that he plays William Tell to do it. He takes aim, and he has the skill to hit the imagined apple and not the real child, just as the child has the wit to understand the allegory, to pick up the hint of danger and the close call. 'Connives' seems somehow to have taken the place of 'contrives', and it's disturbing that taking aim and holding back a tear might look just the same from the other side of the shed. Too many people perhaps have to do both rather too often. The geography of 'past his ear' and 'above his head' is a little strange, but maybe that's how glances split apples. What's clear and very powerful is the logic of the boy's understanding, the precise way he reads the implied story. A shot glance from his father might belong to the old game of Indians, but the splitting apple proves it doesn't. That's the difference between open warfare and redeeming a hostage. This

---

[44] Ibid., 20.

is where we might start thinking about some of the other meanings of 'tell': counting as well as recounting; discerning, as in
'Can we tell the difference'; the usage beautifully defined by the
OED as 'to make known as if by language'; and the way poker
players employ the term to mean the scarcely readable but conclusive expressions or gestures of another player.

   We are in a world recalling that of Seamus Heaney's poems,
where stealth seems to be part of the fabric of a violent reality.
This is a realm of 'neighbourly murder', where a man imagining
a journey to the 'old man-killing parishes' of another country
thinks he will feel lost there, but also 'unhappy and at home'.[45]
And of course stealth also becomes a style. 'Smoke-signals are
loud-mouthed compared with us', Heaney says in a poem elo-
quently entitled 'Whatever You Say Say Nothing'.[46]

   This quiet place, this zone of endless tactical discretion even
when no overt politics are involved, is what Heaney, borrow-
ing a famous phrase from Yeats, calls a singing school.[47] Yeats
thought there was no such school except studying monuments
of the soul's magnificence. At least that's what he said in 'Sailing
to Byzantium', other poems suggest he had other academies too.
Magnificence is a good school, certainly, and no doubt most
poets attend it at some time. But there is also a remarkable col-
lege of constriction and obliquity, where the art of implication is
a core course, and where a whole political history can be shown
in a closed eye—as long as you find the words to suggest what

---

[45]   Seamus Heaney, *Selected Poems 1965–1975* (London: Faber, 1980), 102, 79.
[46]   Seamus Heaney, *North* (London: Faber, 1975), 59.
[47]   *North*, 62–73.

words can't say and what glances can only shoot past you or over you. The camouflage school in the title of a tense and unsettling recent book by Tom Paulin, is not quite a singing school, but there too deceptions are taught, and disguise—in this case of warships during the First World War—creates 'too much ... for the eye to see all at once': like a too-trained ear

> quite unable
> to apportion blame
> or catch at an off-rhyme[48]

In this place you can't hear a whisper, and even William Tell might miss his target.

VI

Dangling, snarling, complacent, miming secrecy and silence, the words of poets circle the question of Ireland and displace and encode the question of violence. Is there too much indirection here, too much submission to the world's doubleness? A good deal of the work of Paul Muldoon's contemporary Eavan Boland is an eloquent plea for direct speech, a refusal of circling and displacement. She repeatedly names the violence; and the scene is unmistakable. *In a Time of Violence* is a volume of poems from 1994, and in 2007 she published a collection called *Domestic Violence*—where 'domestic' means both personal rather than political, and national rather than foreign. We all have our

---

[48] Tom Paulin, *The Camouflage School* (Thame: The Clutag Press, 2007), no page numbers.

histories, and we are all tempted, she suggests in the opening piece in this later book, 'to think the only history [is] our own'. We don't understand, or don't wish to understand, that

> nothing is ever entirely
> right in the lives of those who love each other
> and still less have we
> fathomed what it is
> is wrong in the lives of those who hate each other.

But our failure, Boland suggests, if it is a failure, is partly willed or a failure of will, an occlusion. Perhaps we have already fathomed what we say we can't fathom. 'I think we know. I think we always knew.'[49]

In an earlier poem, 'Beautiful Speech', it seems that language itself bears part of the blame, because it offers us a 'book of satin phrases' that makes it hard for us even to imagine unspoken but never banished words like *hate* and *territory*.

> We will live, we have lived
> where language is concealed. Is perilous.
> We will be—we have been—citizens
> of its hiding place.[50]

And in the later book Boland says of 'the Nineteenth-Century Irish Poets' that

---

[49] Eavan Boland, *Domestic Violence* (Manchester: Carcanet Press, 1999), 11–12.

[50] Eavan Boland, *In a Time of Violence* (Manchester: Carcanet, 1994), 13–14.

> They lived their lives. Kept their counsel. Held their peace.
> But now, looking back, I think they were poisoned—
> every word they used contaminated by the one it was not ...
> Now I see what it is they left us. The toxic lyric.[51]

The verdict seems harsh and we may suspect a touch of the idiom of the old country: every word was a contaminated word. Certainly poets, like everyone else, can lie to us and lie to themselves. Yet they can also—and this is what I have been trying to show throughout this chapter and indeed throughout this book—arrange for words to be *illuminated* by the ones they are not, and by instances that are not words at all. They can project what Henry James calls 'the possible other case',[52] never more necessary to imagine than in a time of violence.

Boland's plea for directness takes concealment as its subject, and can't avoid the necessary tilt of connotation and strategic address. In 'Time and Violence' she says 'we'—she is speaking for women now—do not need poems where the subjects

> languish in a grammar of sighs,
> in the high-minded search for euphony,
> in the midnight rhetoric of poesie.
> 'We cannot sweat here', she continues.
> Our skin is icy.
> We cannot breed here. Our wombs are empty.
> Help us to escape youth and beauty.

---

[51] *Domestic Violence*, 52.
[52] Henry James, *The Art of the Novel* (New York: Scribner's, 1962), 222.

> Write us out of the poem. Make us human
> in cadences of change and mortal pain
> and words we can grow old and die in.[53]

Even here, though, the words rely considerably on what they are not. 'Write us out of the poem', for example, is a fine mock request, a figure of speech. Boland is only pretending to ask for the masculine help she can't have much hope or need of. She is writing herself, skilfully and authoritatively, into a quite different poem.

What's important in all the works I have looked at in this chapter is that they resolutely display a deceived and deceiving world, a given and undeniable reality, and also implicitly make available options which that world cannot currently reach: the minds of actual Irish people hidden beneath the projection of Cromwell's supposed Irish fans; the decency trying to survive disaster in Yeats' poem, the language other than mockery that the poem can't find; the dead culture of pre-Cromwell Ireland; the sharp, individual thought buried beneath the cosy and depressed clichés of the old country; the full range of opportunities afforded by saying nothing; the unspoken idiom that will not collude with the dangers of the hiding place. The poems are giving us an alternative memory. We couldn't imagine these options if the poems didn't suggest them to us. But we do have to take the trouble to imagine them, otherwise they don't really exist. The encounter of writer and reader and poem is itself, or can be, a model of sympathetic, many-angled work and play, and a liveable answer to the violence of pacifying rule and the violence of refusing to recognize any rule at all.

[53] *In a Time of Violence*, 50.

Close reading means reading what's not there as well as what is, and understanding the contamination of words in as many senses, good and bad, as possible. We might risk an answer to Yeats' rhetorical questions, 'What more is there to say', 'What is there left to say'. There may be nothing left to say, but the unsaid leaves us plenty to do. Wittgenstein didn't quite propose, as he is often supposed to have done, that what can't be said can be shown. He remarked, of the sentence 'There are natural laws', that of course (*freilich*) one cannot say that, and added, 'It shows itself'.[54] Poems do plenty of saying and revealing and hinting, but they also create spaces where history and its lost shadows, even in their resistance to anything resembling natural laws, vividly show themselves.

[54] Ludwig Wittgenstein, *Tractatus Logico-Philosophicus*, trans. C. K. Ogden (London: Routledge, 1999), 176–7.

5

Violence Upon The Roads

The current amazement that the things we are experiencing are 'still' possible in the twentieth century is *not* philosophical.

WALTER BENJAMIN, *'On the Concept of History'*

I

In 1934 Marina Tsvetaeva wrote an essay called 'Poets with History
and Poets without History' ['Poety s istoriei i poety bez istorii'].
All poets, she said, belong to one or the other of these categories,
and it becomes clear that the poet with history—her examples are
Goethe and Pushkin—is there for the contrast, that her aim is to
talk about, even justify, the existence of the poet without history.
The poet with history is either defunct or everywhere, and therefore scarcely a poet at all; the poet without history is an enigma
or a dissident. The poet without history resists history, as Roland
Barthes once said it was the business of literature in general to do.
The literary work, he argued, is 'at once the sign of a history and
resistance to that history' ('à la fois signe d'une histoire et résistance

à cette histoire').[1] Another way of describing Tsvetaeva's essay would be to say that she wants to talk to us about the (probably advantageous) narrowing, over time, of poetry into lyric poetry; about the situation in which 'poetry' has simply come to mean the lyric, while the long poem, or the epic poem, or the novel in verse all need special names and special advertising.

Poets with history discover themselves through discovering the world. 'They walk without turning round ... Had the mature Goethe met the young Goethe at a crossroads, he might actually have failed to recognise him and might have sought to make his acquaintance ... Poets with history are, above all, poets of a theme. We always know what they are writing about ... Rarely are they pure lyricists ... Poets with history are, above all, poets of will.'[2]

'Pure lyric poetry has no project,' Tsvetaeva says. She adds that there is nothing more boring than hearing other people's dreams, but when a poet tells you his or her dream—her examples are Mandelstam, Akhmatova, Pasternak—the dream is fascinating because it is also your own. Lyric poets, she says, 'came into the world not to learn, but to say. To say what they already know: everything they know (if it is a lot) or the only thing they know (if it is just one thing) ... The poet with history never knows what is going to happen to him. The pure lyricist always knows that nothing is going to happen to him, that he will have nothing but himself: his own tragic lyric experience.'[3]

[1] Roland Barthes, 'Histoire ou littérature', in *Sur Racine* (Paris: Seuil, 1963), 149.

[2] Marina Tsvetaeva, *Art in the Light of Conscience*, trans. Angela Livingstone (Cambridge, Mass.: Harvard University Press, 1992), 137.

[3] Ibid. 139, 140, 142.

Are there no exceptions, no crossovers, no poets who manage to be both with and without history? There is one: Alexander Blok, 'a pure lyricist who did have development and history and a path.' But then Tsvetaeva corrects herself almost immediately. 'Development' is not the word she wants. 'Development presupposes harmony. Can there be a development which is—catastrophic? And can there be harmony when what we see is a soul being torn completely apart?'[4]

Yeats is undeniably a poet devoted to his own tragic lyric experience, and when the mature Yeats met the young Yeats at a crossroads, as he frequently did, he certainly recognized him. If in 'Nineteen Hundred and Nineteen', first published in 1921, we learn that 'the Platonic Year | Whirls out new right and wrong', and that 'all men are dancers and their tread | Goes to the barbarous clangour of a gong', it was already the case in 'The Song of the Happy Shepherd' of 1889 that there were

> many changing things
> In dreary dancing past us whirled,
> To the cracked tune that Chronos sings.[5]

But Yeats was surely also a poet of will, and of an identifiable cluster of themes; and since it seems implausible anyway to claim a dramatist, autobiographer, essayist, and writer of fiction as a 'pure lyricist', we should perhaps just move Yeats to the other

---

[4] Marina Tsvetaeva, *Art in the Light of Conscience*, trans. Angela Livingstone (Cambridge, Mass.: Harvard University Press, 1992), 148.

[5] *Variorium Edition*, 65. This connection was pointed out long ago by Michael Ragussis in *The Subterfuge of Art*.

camp, that of the poets with history, and line him up happily with Goethe and Pushkin, not bad company after all. And yet such a move would lose us something, the chance of a different insight. For if Blok found a catastrophic way of linking the lyric with history, tearing himself apart in the process, Yeats, I suggest, sought to use the lyric as, among other things, a survivable way of understanding history. As if the lyric, the mind talking musically to itself, were finally the best instrument left for hearing both the damage and the music of the world. A woman in Belfast in one of the finest poems in Tom Paulin's *Invasion Handbook*

> hands her dream on
> to her eldest son
> who wonders if mere dreams
> can weigh in the record
> or for that matter can poems?[6]

Both poems and dreams, lyric poems and mere dreams, can weigh in the record—if we are lucky they *are* the record, they remember and reflect on what can't be thought otherwise.

II

A lyric poet with history might actually create an event for the record. On one of the occasions when the mature Yeats met his younger self at a crossroads he asked a question that has been much quoted and brilliantly mocked.

[6] Tom Paulin, *The Invasion Handbook* (London: Faber and Faber, 2002), 144.

> Did that play of mine send out
> Certain men the English shot?[7]

The question appears in the poem 'The Man and the Echo', and the play—by Yeats and Lady Gregory, as it happened—is *Cathleen ni Houlihan*, first performed in Dublin in 1902. An imagined W. H. Auden, in a poem by Paul Muldoon, has a sharp, rhyming answer: 'Certainly not'. Denis Donoghue, picking up this challenge in an article, says the answer is certainly not 'certainly not', because it is 'entirely possible that some members of the audience … felt impelled to take up arms in a nationalist cause already well established'.[8] Stephen Gwynn, writing in 1936 of his memory of the first production, asked himself 'if such plays should be produced unless one was prepared for people to go out and shoot and be shot'.[9]

The poem's question is too directly causal to be taken literally, and this is why Donoghue's double negative seems the ideal grammatical approach. The play didn't send out Irishmen to be shot because those men had choices of their own to make, they were not the simple children of propaganda. But the play certainly contributed to the elaboration of the moral climate in which those men made their choices.

Muldoon's first take on Yeats is very funny but a little later in the same poem the voice of an imagined Louis MacNeice gives

[7] W. B. Yeats, *The Variorum Edition of the Poems*, ed. Peter Allt and Russell K. Alspach (New York: Macmillan, 1957), 632.

[8] Denis Donoghue, 'Yeats: The New Political Issue', *Princeton University Library Chronicle* (Spring 1998), 364.

[9] Quoted in Richard J. Finneran (ed.), *The Collected Poems of W. B. Yeats* (New York: Scribner, 1996), 544.

us a strong counterblast to the imagined Auden's view, and recalls
Yeats in a different mode. Here's what Auden is said to say. He is
called simply 'Wystan', and the poem in question is titled '7 Midd-
agh Street', after an address in Brooklyn where a host of artists
and writers (including Auden, Carson McCullers, Jane and Paul
Bowles, Benjamin Britten, and Gypsy Rose Lee) lived in 1940.

> And were Yeats living at this hour
> it should be in some ruined tower
>
> not malachited Ballylee
> where he paid out to those below
>
> one gilt-edged scroll from his pencil
> as though he were part Rapunzel
>
> and partly Delphic oracle.
> As for his crass rhetorical
>
> posturing, 'Did that play of mine
> send out certain men (*certain* men?)
>
> the English shot ...?
> The answer is 'Certainly not'.
>
> If Yeats had saved his pencil-lead
> would certain men have stayed in bed?
>
> For history's a twisted root
> with art its small, translucent fruit
>
> and never the other way round.[10]

---

[10] Paul Muldoon, *Selected Poems 1968–1986* (Farrar, Straus and Giroux, 1993), 134.

And here, in the voice of 'Louis' is an answer to the assertion that poetry, or a play, makes nothing happen:

> In dreams begin responsibilities:
> it was on account of just such an allegory
> that Lorca
> was riddled with bullets
>
> and lay mouth down
> in the fickle shadow of his own blood.
> As the drunken soldiers of the *Gypsy Ballads*
> started back for town
>
> they heard him calling through the mist,
> 'When I die leave the balcony shutters open.'
> For poetry *can* make things happen—
> not only can, but *must*—[11]

Must, and does, since it gets Lorca killed, in a disreputable local version of reprisals. Both 'Auden' and MacNeice' are anxious about poetry and history, the one desperately eager not to claim too much for art, and taking Yeats as the arch-culprit in the vatic overselling of the trade, the other not sure that poetry helps us but sure it can do damage or lead to terrible harm. 'In dreams begin responsibilities' is the title story of a book by Delmore Schwartz (published in 1938), who is mentioned a little earlier in the Muldoon poem, and it looks back to Yeats' possibly invented epigraph to his book of poems called *Responsibilities*: 'In dreams begins responsibility'.

---

[11] *Selected Poems*, 152.

And we recognize the soldiers of course not from Lorca's *Gypsy Ballads* but from Yeats' 'Nineteen Hundred and Nineteen'. They are *the* drunken soldiers now, not *a* drunken soldiery, members of the Nationalist militia proceeding to an execution rather than indulging in a drive-by shooting. The year is 1936, the place is Víznar, near Granada. But the execution is scrambled and (probably) unauthorized, the confused creation of turbulence itself, and Muldoon/MacNeice's point is clear. Lorca was killed because he was a poet, and the soldiers who killed him came from a poem. That poem itself came from history, from 'the present state of the world', and history, specific as it always is, can travel like a poem. A drunken soldiery, or even sober but enraged soldiers, can murder not only the mother but also the poet, and they can do their work in Spain just as callously and recklessly as in Ireland. They even appear, a little ahead of time and rather calmer but already drunk, in a poem by Ciaran Carson about World War I.[12] And yet Lorca, like Eileen or Ellen Quinn, like the victims of mustard gas Carson evokes, like all of us, will die only once.

What 'Wystan' and 'Louis' taken together are saying is that the effects of poetry are always oblique and often belated, but can be real and indeed devastating. A play or a poem sends no one out, but neither can it recall or deny those who go out in its name. Poetry makes nothing happen but its drunken soldiers are always on the move.

Or its sacrificial victims. In *Cathleen ni Houlihan* Michael Gillane is to be married. The girl is lovely, the dowry is substantial,

---

[12] 'The drunken soldiery had taken to the bed': Ciaran Carson, 'Mustard', *The Twelfth of Never* (London: Picador, 1999), 69.

his parents are delighted. But then a French expeditionary force lands in Ireland, and hopes to recruit likely locals for the war against the English. The year is 1798. At the same time a 'strange woman' appears on the road. She is said to be the person who 'goes through the country the time there's war or trouble coming'. But she is more than that, she is Ireland herself, harried by the presence of 'too many strangers in the house', and mourning the loss of the 'four beautiful green fields' that make up her identity. 'Some call me the Poor Old Woman', she says, 'and there are some that call me Cathleen ni Houlihan'. 'Many a man has died for love of me', she insists. 'There were a great many in the West, some that died hundreds of years ago, and there are some that will die tomorrow.' She has 'good friends', she says, meaning partly the French and mainly all the Irishmen who will fight for her. She says she has hopes ('The hope of getting my beautiful fields back again; the hope of putting the strangers out of my house'), but it is not these vague and indeed for so long poorly founded hopes that make her irresistible. It is the 'hard service' she requires of her lovers. She represents not a death wish but a temptation to self-sacrifice for which death may be the only true conclusion. Michael Gillane leaves his bride and his family and goes off to follow the old woman—although as she steps down the path she doesn't look like an old woman any more. Michael's younger brother watches her go, and says he 'saw a young girl, and she had the walk of a queen'.[13]

[13] W. B. Yeats, *Collected Plays* (London and Basingstoke: Macmillan, 1982), 76, 81, 85; 82, 83, 84, 86, 88.

Cathleen is not entirely irresistible. In the play, no one but Michael is moved by her plight or even understands what she is talking about. But her attraction is very real, and anyone may feel it who has ever wanted to give themselves to a cause or a person without any expectation of reward or return. Cathleen understands the deep secret of such desires. She says:

It is a hard service they take that help me. Many that are red-cheeked now will be pale-cheeked; many that have been free to walk the hills and the bogs and the rushes will be sent to walk hard streets in far countries; many a good plan will be broken; many that have gathered money will not stay to spend it; many a child will be born and there will be no father at its christening to give it a name. They that had red cheeks will have pale cheeks for my sake; and for all that they will think they are well paid.[14]

This is I think the voice of the lyric in prose. A persona is speaking, of course, as in all of Yeats' lyrics, but the form is that of sung thought rather than dramatic interaction. Cathleen is not saying that the service is hard but a help towards a distant victory, a gesture of 'self-sacrifice for the common good', as Richard Taylor puts it[15]—even though this may be what she means in terms of her mission. She is saying that the hardness of the service is what it's all about, and that such service is itself a vocation. Pale cheeks, hard streets, broken plans, unspent money, fatherless children: a picture of sacrifice for sacrifice's sake, and virtually irresistible

[14] Ibid. 86.
[15] Richard Taylor, *A Reader's Guide to the Plays of W. B. Yeats* (New York: St Martin's Press, 1984), 33.

if we are at all this way inclined. The struggle in the play, Yeats said in an interview, is 'against all that we mean when we say the world'.[16] In this context what we mean when we say the world is a place where we might be happy or comfortable, might live the life Michael Gillane abandons, and Yeats understands perfectly how eager a noble soul might be to renounce it.

A noble soul? Yes, because surely the appeal, for all its dangerous consequences in history, is to a noble aspiration, a desire to give as well as a desire to give up. What Yeats is asking in his later poem, perhaps, is what it means to have pitched so perfectly a myth that claimed so many hearts, even if the myth is clearly not (certainly not) of his own inventing. And if Yeats, long after the initial production of the play and in spite of substantial disagreements with militant Irish nationalists, finds himself, as Terence Brown puts it, 'in imaginative understanding' of Patrick Pearse, one of the heroes and martyrs of 1916, it was because Pearse himself, as Brown goes on subtly to say, 'had followed the summons of a young woman with the walk of a queen'.[17] That is, Yeats could understand Pearse without sharing his politics because Pearse's politics were based on the myth Yeats had so deeply construed. And if Yeats came as he did to think Pearse was 'a dangerous man' driven by 'the vertigo of self-sacrifice', he could scarcely deny his own contribution to the vertigo.[18] Pearse

[16] Quoted in A. Norman Jeffares and A. S. Knowland, *A Commentary on the Collected Plays of W. B. Yeats* (Stanford: Stanford University Press, 1975), 27.

[17] Terence Brown, *The Life of W. B. Yeats* (Oxford: Blackwell, 1999), 276.

[18] Ruth Dudley Edwards, *Patrick Pearse: the Triumph of Failure* (Dublin and Portland, Oregon: Irish Academic Press, 2006), 335.

indeed grasped and made explicit what I have just suggested is the lyric meaning of the play: 'A love and a service so excessive as to annihilate all thought of self, a recognition that one must give all'. Heroes are to 'turn their backs to the pleasant paths and their faces to the hard paths, to blind their eyes to the fair things of life'.[19] This is what he said in 1913 in a speech commemorating Wolfe Tone. Not just a complete love and service, we note, but an excessive love and service. Nothing less than excess will be enough, and that is precisely the appeal of Cathleen ni Houlihan.

All this has resulted, as everyone knows, in what F. S. L. Lyons calls a 'dire obsession'. 'It has been too easy', Lyons writes, 'to analyse the Irish question not just in political terms but in terms of the politics of violence.'[20] Hence Lyons' own turn to the question of culture. But this is where violence reappears, and reappears in just the story we are looking at. One commentator has suggested that Pearse's imagery shows 'an almost pathological lust for violence'.[21] His imagery, we note. Does the violence have to reappear? It does once you have made the connection between sacrifice and bloodshed seem inevitable, as Pearse and Yeats, and finally even James Connolly did.

> 'But where can we draw water,'
> Said Pearse to Connolly,

[19] Quoted in F. S. Lyons, *Culture and Anarchy in Ireland 1890–1939* (Oxford: Clarendon Press, 1979), 88.

[20] *Culture and Anarchy in Ireland*, 90, 1.

[21] William Irwin Thompson, quoted in Charles Townshend, *Easter 1916: The Irish Rebellion* (London: Penguin, 2006), 23.

> 'When all the wells are parched away?
> O plain as plain can be
> There's nothing but our own red blood
> Can make a right Rose Tree.'[22]

This is horribly appealing because it combines what appears to be hard-line practical politics, getting something done, with sacrificial exaltation. And sometimes you can just have the bloodshed and leave the sacrifice implied. 'We may make mistakes in the beginning', Pearse famously wrote in 'The Coming Revolution', 'and shoot the wrong people; but bloodshed is a cleansing and a sanctifying thing.' Roy Foster shrewdly names the reader's options: 'This might variously be interpreted as sinister gibberish, Swiftian irony or the rational reaction to the terms set by Ulster.'[23] However we take it, the violence is to be redeemed by the sheer selflessness of its performance. Geoffrey Wheatcroft, in an obituary for Conor Cruise O'Brien, tells us that 'this lifelong anti-clerical said once that he would always choose Holy Mother Church over Cathleen ni Houlihan with her crueller kind of sterile blood-sacrifice.'[24] This is an impressive choice but in 1916 many more or less orthodox Catholics may have felt the two divinities were much the same, and Connolly himself compared the situation of the Irish rebels to that of 'mankind before Calvary', waiting not for turbulence but for the 'shedding of blood' and the consequent redemption.[25]

---

[22] *Variorum Edition*, 396.

[23] R. F. Foster, *Modern Ireland 1600–1972* (London Penguin, 1989), 477.

[24] Geoffrey Wheatcroft, 'Conor Cruise O'Brien', *New York Review of Books*, 26 March 2009.

[25] *Culture and Anarchy in Ireland*, 90.

Lyons reminds us that this spirit, so often seen as a peculiar Irish glory or pathology, was part of a wider European mentality; and however closely sacrifice and bloodshed are associated, they are logically and morally separable. Self-sacrifice, for example, has no automatic connection with shedding anyone else's red blood. In 1916, Pearse himself surrendered in order to save the lives of others, and Charles Townshend reports a moving story of a slippage between a general indication and an individual life. When asked during the Rebellion whether looters were to be shot, Pearse said yes. Presented with a particular looter, Pearse said, 'Ah, poor man, just keep him with the others.'[26]

There are haunting Catholic versions of the sacrifice story in the work of Paul Claudel; there is a strong Protestant version in the later work of Thomas Mann. In both cases the emphasis, as in *Cathleen ni Houlihan* and in Pearse's speeches, is on diffi-culty—or rather on whatever is caught, in French or German or English, by the words 'hard' or 'dur' or 'schwer'. 'There's a hard wind outside,' the old woman says in the play. All of these words mean difficult, but 'dur', like 'hard', has an implication of density, physical resistance, harshness; and 'schwer' means heavy as well. J. P. Stern's book *The Dear Purchase* magisterially traces this form of thinking in German literature. His title is a literal translation of the phrase 'der teure Kauf', and somewhere lurking in the idea is the suggestion that even Christ might have paid too much for the redemption of humanity.[27] That is, only through paying too

[26] *Easter 1916*, 264.

[27] J. P. Stern, *The Dear Purchase* (Cambridge: Cambridge University Press, 1995), *passim*, and esp. 363–1.

much could he pay enough, settle that whole appalling human account. The Protestant *Book of Common Prayer*, quoting the 31st of the 39 Articles, says Christ paid exactly the right amount, not a drop of blood too much or too little: 'The offering of Christ once made is the perfect redemption, propitiation, and satisfaction for all the sins of the whole world, both original and actual, and there is no other satisfaction for sin but that alone.' Christ really did redeem us, but the text still sounds a little worried, on two fronts: perhaps the dear purchase was not quite enough, and perhaps the perfect kindness of Christ could be expressed only through an excess of sacrifice.

Stern finds versions of the appeal to self-loss in all kinds of places, notably in the ending of Mann's *Dr Faustus*, where the composer Adrian Leverkühn, having summoned his friends to hear him play from his most recent work, addresses the company in a parody of Luther's German. Among other things, Leverkühn insists that he has not been easy on himself, but has lived 'according to the word of the Apostle: "He who seeketh hard things shall have it hard"'. A little later he says 'Perchance God sees, too, that I sought out what was hard and gave myself to drudgery, perchance, perchance it may be reckoned to me and put to my account that I have been so diligent and complished all with pertinacity.'[28] This is the man who has sold his soul to the devil and knows his twenty-four years are up: the Protestant work ethic in extremis. Surely in any other theology working hard on behalf of the devil would be worse than slacking. Here

[28] Thomas Mann, *Doctor Faustus*, trans. John E. Woods (New York: Vintage, 1999), 525–6.

any form of difficulty, if diligently adhered to, offers at least a fantasy of salvation. Anything that costs so much can't be bad. Or even: anything that costs so much makes you a hero.

This is surely the view that Yeats is revoking in 'Easter 1916'. 'Too long a sacrifice | Can make a stone of the heart'.[29] Sacrifice can be measured, there can be too much of it. And the poet's question in the next line—'O when may it suffice?'—with its helpless logic and its troubling rhyme on the two key words clearly denies the infinite attraction of the old hard service which delighted in excesses of renunciation.

I called the association of sacrifice and bloodshed horribly appealing, and I do think it's helpful to separate the two. But the doctrine of justification through difficulty I have just described, although perhaps more appealing, is finally not less horrible, because in spite of all the appearances of selflessness it exalts the sovereign striving self above everything else and banishes the world; and if it doesn't require bloodshed it doesn't exclude it either, because it doesn't exclude anything, even the thought that a pact with the devil wouldn't prevent you from occupying a portion of the moral high ground.

It seems that in its modern version this story is the exact contemporary of the mentality I evoked earlier in this book, the mentality of the late Victorian and Edwardian era, pre-war in England, pre-Rebellion in Ireland, represented or ventriloquized as a 'we' who had thought the world to be 'gradually bettering', in Henry James' phrase, or who, in the words of Yeats' 'Nineteen Hundred and Nineteen', had 'pieced our thoughts into philoso-

---

[29] *Variorum Edition*, 394.

phy | And planned to bring the world under a rule'. In the man-
uscript Yeats spells pieced as 'peaced'—a nice touch, although
it's hard to know whether to attribute it to a Freudian slip or
poor spelling. It's certainly a good verb for not learning war any
more, which is what the poem's reference to ploughshares and to
Isaiah 2: 4 suggests: 'neither shall they learn war any more.' Now
we see that alongside these (perhaps imaginary and certainly
schematized) people who believed in the rules and (wrongly)
thought the rules were working, there was a second group con-
sisting of those who knew all along that the world was rotten,
that the rules were an easy illusion, that the world as it was had
to be renounced, and that the only salvation lay in a stricter, piti-
less requirement, the hard regime of perpetual sacrifice. There is
a third mentality too, more plainly a part of Yeats' picture than
of James', which lurks within or behind the other two, and which
rests on a fascinated horror of, or a horrified fascination with,
the very idea of a world without rules. This mentality relies for
its emblems on other figures, drunken soldiers in Ireland or in
Spain, evil spirits returning from Kilkenny and the fourteenth
century, Greek gods, dead members of a German army, Russian
troops in the midst of revolution, who all embody a violence
without grounds and without restraint, and who pay no sort of
penalty.

It may be worth pausing over the word 'can' in the lines in
'Nineteen Hundred and Nineteen' that describe the actions of
'a drunken soldiery'.[30] It's as if the implied phrase 'How could

---

[30] In his drafts for the poem Yeats twice wrote 'may' and each time
changed it to 'can'. *The Tower,* edited by Richard J Finneran, 200, 218.

they' shifts from shocked rhetorical question into a historical enigma: 'Well, how could they?' The nightmare concerns not only what the soldiers do but what they permit themselves—or are permitted—to do. They

> Can leave the mother, murdered at her door,
> To crawl in her own blood, and go scot-free;

The going scot-free is as important, sadly, as the woman's death, and an atrocious liberty finds its expression here. 'One thing I did not foresee,' Yeats wrote in 1921, 'not having the courage of my own thought: the growing murderousness of the world.'[31] The world is murderous by nature perhaps, and perhaps always was; but it has become more murderous still because it allows and even encourages murder.

III

The second passage of named violence in 'Nineteen Hundred and Nineteen', and the only occurrences of the word itself, appear at the end of the poem—'Violence upon the roads: violence of horses'—and announce a new and perhaps monstrous dispensation. The suggestion is that the two violences—the historical nightmare and the apocalyptic vision—are intimately connected. It is because we cannot deal with the first, cannot coherently live with the news it seems to bring, that we find ourselves, in an ugly, excitable mood of fake reluctance, half-awaiting the second. As I suggested earlier, this is a key moment

[31] W. B. Yeats, *Autobiographies* (New York: Scribner, 1999), 166.

in so many of Yeats' poems: just before. The Magi are poised for a second turn of turbulence, alert for whatever echo they may find for the literally earth-shaking events of Christ's Calvary. The rough beast of 'The Second Coming' hasn't reached Bethlehem and isn't born yet, but its cruel Christmas can't be far off.

Violence upon the roads recalls the drunken soldiery, of course, if only by implication. The mother in Part I of the poem was 'murdered at her door', the soldiers were presumably driving or stumbling past on the street. But then the violent horses shift the picture. The soldiers could have been riding them in the poem if not in the historical Ireland of the reference, but the shifted epithet still seems strange, and horses that are themselves violent transform both the drowsy chargers of Part I and the nightmare that rides upon sleep. Yeats' refusal to specify the violence creates an especially alarming effect, like the vagueness in a Henry James ghost story. Are the horses kicking, rearing, biting, stampeding? No, just ... violent.

These horses are a visitation, a supernatural army it seems. In his note Yeats mentions 'apparitions' that 'the country people' see and call either 'fallen angels' or 'ancient inhabitants of the country'. The people also sometimes see 'flowers upon the heads of the horses', a view which gives us the garlands of the second line of this part of the poem, and presumably suggests the 'delicate sensitive ear or tossing mane'. But there is a slight slippage between Yeats' comment and the poem, since what the country people see are horsemen, and in the poem only 'some few' of the horses have handsome riders. Perhaps the rest of the horses have unhandsome riders (and no garlands), but the stronger implication, following on from the stark phrase 'violence of horses' is that the rest of the herd is riderless, not even dragon-ridden. Whose horses are they? Who are the handsome riders? What does it mean to be handsome in such a world, such a vision? We know only that the horses are weary, that they run in circles. And that they vanish.

Now the blind daughters of Herodias appear, or more precisely, 'have returned again'. Are they riding horses too—the phrase 'thunder of feet' may suggest this, but 'tumult of images' warns us against looking for anything too graphically precise. You would have to be crazy to mess with any of them, obviously, but someone does, since 'should' (in the line 'And should some crazy hand dare touch a daughter') loses its conditionality almost as soon as it is spoken—*all* the daughters respond when one of them is approached. They respond, in another of Yeats' calculated ambiguities, with 'amorous cries or angry cries'. Perhaps some of the daughters are amorous and others are angry. Or all their cries are either amorous or angry, a mere mortal listener is not going to be able to tell. The syntax adds its own bit of shiftiness here by suggesting that the cries are amorous or angry 'according to the wind', but when the sentence settles down we realize that this is not the case; that the daughters 'turn ... according to the wind', because they are blind, and are hearing each other's cries erratically. But who are the daughters of Herodias? And what is 'their purpose in the labyrinth of the wind'?

Writing about a much earlier poem, Yeats associates these figures with 'the gods of ancient Ireland' who 'still ride the country as of old'. These gods sometimes called the Sidhe, a word which 'is also Gaelic for wind', Yeats explains, 'and certainly the Sidhe have much to do with the wind. They journey in whirling winds,

the winds that were called the dance of the daughters of Herodias in the Middle Ages, Herodias doubtless taking the place of
some old goddess.[32] Doubtless. By the Middle Ages Herodias
had, according to Montague Summers, become 'a witchqueen
who called the sorcerers together to meetings … by night, when
they feasted, sacrificed babes to ghouls and ghosts.[33] This seems
a lot further than the daughters are going in the poem, with
their bewildered, ambiguous cries, and what's interesting in the
image is perhaps less the hint of witchcraft than the slippage
away from even ghostly literality or personhood; and the sheer
multiplicity of the creatures. They journey in the winds, and it
is the winds that are called, not the daughters of Herodias but
the dance of those daughters. The daughters are metaphorical
figures in a dance that is already a metaphor for the wind. But
the dance does of course evoke the most famous of Herodias'
daughters, Salome, and her fatal interest in the head of John the
Baptist. It is possible, as Jeffares notes, that Herodias took 'the
place of some old goddess,[34] because the dance of the winds was
associated with a particular date, 24 June, the feast of St John,
but in any case the effect of the allusion or the conflation of figures is to conjure up both art and death, or more precisely death
(someone else's death) as a reward for art.

In all the famous versions of the story of Salome, from
Flaubert to Mallarmé to Wilde, there is only one woman, and
Yeats has borrowed, and intensified the idea of the plural from

---

[32] *Variorum Edition*, 800.
[33] *A New Commentary*, 234.
[34] Ibid., 234.

Arthur Symons' poem 'The Dance of the Daughters of Herodias'. There is something very striking, even daunting, about
this multiplication of Salomes, and about their appearance in
a crowd on the road rather than in a palace, a second act to a
herd of violent horses. Symons' poem is slack and misty, and
his conception of the femme fatale hopelessly conventional.
Even so, the idea that Salome is everywhere, and that there is no
shortage of men to play the role of John the Baptist at any time,
has its edgy touch of fear, just because the original story seemed
so strange and specific.

> I see a pale and windy multitude
> Beaten about the air, as if the smoke
> Of incense kindled into invisible life
> Shadowy and invisible presences;
> And, in the cloudy darkness, I can see
> The thin white feet of many women dancing ...
>
>   ...each of them
> Carries a beautiful platter in her hand,
> Smiling, because she holds against her heart
> The secret lips and unresting brow
> Some John the Baptist's head makes lamentable ...
>
> Pale, windy, and ecstatic multitude
> Beaten about this mortal air ...[35]

And their purpose? Well, how do we parse the single complicated sentence describing them? The syntactical frame is clear:

[35] Arthur Symons, 'The Dance of the Daughters of Herodias', in *Images
of Good and Evil* (Poole and New York: Woodstock Books, 1996), 42, 48.

'Herodias' daughters have returned again … and should some crazy hand dare touch a daughter all turn with amorous cries, or angry cries, according to the wind, for all are blind.' But then the parenthesis—'a sudden blast of dusty wind and after thunder of feet, tumult of images, their purpose in the labyrinth of the wind'—although powerfully descriptive and evocative, has a kind of semantic dissolve in its last clause. What is their purpose in the labyrinth of the wind? Do we read the parenthesis as saying 'there was a sudden blast of dusty wind, and after thunder of feet there came a tumult of images, which was their purpose in the labyrinth of the wind'? Are the thunder of feet and the tumult of images both part of their purpose? Or do we read 'after thunder of feet and tumult of images, they found their (unspecified) purpose in the labyrinth of the wind'? Yeats likes this kind of unmarked parenthesis—there is a fine instance in 'Sailing to Byzantium'—but he doesn't usually have it fall in upon itself in this way. The important effect, I think, is the naming of purpose when purpose can't really be identified. The daughters of Herodias have a goal but we can scarcely comprehend the notion of these blind phantoms having such a thing. We recognize that they could be the sign of a purpose; or they could be actors within a purposeful, apocalyptic event. But the poem says 'their purpose', and leaves us worried, and haunted.

Then the haunting ends. Or rather begins in earnest. Wind drops, dust settles. I have already said something about the compacted consonants of these lines, and their rhythm; and the curious sense that by the time Robert Artisson appears, he seems to be a person we already know. The syntactical delay ('there lurches past ... that ... Robert Artissson') and his arrival at the end of a line are of course part of the tremendous effect. Yeats' imagination is at the end of its tether, as I have suggested, but his skills are intact. Here as often in Yeats there is something almost too fine and too grand about the poetic performance; and here as elsewhere, this hint of imposture turns out to work in the poem's favour, that is, to add to its trouble. Before we hear the spirit's name we see his lurch, his 'great eyes without thought', his 'stupid straw-pale locks', and we hear a condemnation ('that insolent fiend') that seems strangely personal, as if his insolence were more of a problem than his fiendish nature. This is certainly a second coming, since we are in 1919 (or 1921), and Robert Artisson has travelled here from the fourteenth century. But what is he doing, what is his 'purpose' in the calm that follows the fading of the labyrinth of the wind? He doesn't talk, he doesn't think—I don't believe we are meant to imagine his great eyes are *temporarily* without thought, this must be their ordinary condition, a suggestion confirmed by his 'stupid' blonde hair—he doesn't turn or shout, like Herodias' daughters, or do whatever the violent horses are doing to earn their epithet. He just ... passes. He didn't come for us or to us, he lurches by like an image from an old jerky movie, and the poem ends, not on this image, but on a touch of documentary detail about one of his admirers.

The great critical question is why this scene is not the anticlimax it sounds as if it ought to be; and why we can't get Robert Artisson and Lady Kyteler out of our heads. Of course they bring a message, as the daughters and the horses do—or rather we have to read the sight of them, their crossing of our blocked path, as a message of some sort. But the meaning of the evil spirit and the lady must be different from those of their forerunners and announcers, their evangelists, so to speak. They are the thing itself, they are what happens when the wind drops and the dust settles. They are what we were waiting for, and they are … I want to suggest three not quite compatible interpretations. They just are the revelation they are supposed to be, because *anything* would be a revelation after such a build-up, as long as it avoided mere familiarity or bathos, and these two figures certainly do that. Or they are more than that, *a* second coming, if not *the* second coming, and all second comings are spiritually respectable, whatever their moral status—it's not nothing to have survived six centuries and to have a starring role in the pageant of what some think are the last days of humankind. And/or finally they represent undying power and desire, the ability to enchant and the longing to be enchanted, a world of magical dominion and magical sacrifice—where even vain gifts, those peacock feathers and those cocks' red combs, for example, to which Artisson probably pays about as much attention as he does to Yeats or to us, enact real obsession and devotion. This is what it means for the poem to end, not with Artisson and not even with Lady Kyteler, but with her offerings. There aren't even any birds here, just feathers and crests, whatever it takes for desperation to find a formal, ritual expression.

Helen Vendler catches a good deal of this mood when she writes of 'the sexual satisfaction' that is 'the origin of human violence', but we can, I think, go one frightening step further. The subject is definitely sex, but there is no satisfaction, only endless desire, and there is no immediate violence, only the intimation that violence could happen any moment, and is likely to be all the more catastrophic because of the appearance of calm. The mindless power of Robert Artisson, not in itself sexual, but working through the sexual passion of others, will be the source of any turbulence to come. The terror of the rough beast in 'The Second Coming' lies both in the new order it will bring, the end of a cycle, and the almost certainly violent means it will use in the bringing. Robert Artisson's promises are different. There will be no new order, only the incoherent dying of the old, and our disarray is such that we may find ourselves, against our will, shifting into a version of the role of the abject Lady Kyteler. We may be half in love not with Artisson or even what he represents, but with whatever terminal disasters he can wreak or conjure, whatever havoc a 600-year-old spirit without mind or conscience can let loose upon the world. It is possible, as we know from a remark by Yeats himself, to delight in the failure of the myth of progress. The sentiment here is not only the angry disappointment of Part I of 'Nineteen Hundred and Nineteen' but something like an excitable form of historical *Schadenfreude*. 'When I was a boy', Yeats wrote, 'rebellion took the form of aversion to that myth [of progress]. I took satisfaction in certain public disasters, felt a sort of ecstasy at the contemplation of ruin.'[36] It would be nice to think we don't understand him. The horror is that Artisson does not represent only horror, any more than the drunken soldiers represent only disorder.

---

[36] Quoted in Helen Vendler, *Yeats's Vision and the Later Plays* (Cambridge, Mass.: Harvard, 1963), 99.

IV

Yeats didn't write 'Nineteen Hundred and Nineteen' in 1919, but he did write 'The Second Coming' in January of that real and symbolic year. Terence Brown reminds us that the manuscripts connect the work to the Treaty of Brest-Litovsk and to a whole series of events, in Ireland and elsewhere, belonging to 'this monumental month'.[37] When I first read the poem, first met the so often quoted lines—

> The best lack all conviction, while the worst
> Are full of passionate intensity—

I was sure it referred to the 1930s, to fascism and appeasement, to Hitler and Mussolini and Chamberlain. And when I learned its date I was baffled. The poem seemed so completely on target for what I thought was its topic.[38] But I finally got used to being wrong, and I knew there was passionate intensity (and lack of conviction) all over the place in 1919 too. We do need to return to the question of shifting reference, though. There are many ways in which a poem can be 'about' something—even more,

[37] Terence Brown reminds us that the manuscripts connect the poem to the Treaty of Brest-Litovsk and to a whole series of events belonging to January 1919, 'this monumental month', as Brown says, of this real and symbolic year. *The Life of W. B. Yeats,* 270.

[38] The poem was on target in one sense, of course, and still is. A moment after writing (or rewriting) these words, I read Paul Krugman, in the *New York Times,* August 7, 2009, discussing the president's health care plan and saying that 'Mr Obama's backers seem to lack all conviction. ... Meanwhile, the angry right is filled with a passionate intensity'. Krugman didn't feel he had to indicate the source of the line.

fortunately, than the number of ways in which poems are not 'about' anything. This issue in turn relates to the workings of language more generally, so that what happens in a poem can be seen as a complication or refinement or loosening of those workings. 'How does language hook on to the world?' Wittgenstein famously asked. One answer is that it never does, quite. Another would be that it does it in all kinds of ways, and that particular contexts determine how the act of hooking works, so that at this moment you know, for various contingent but sufficient reasons, that the Wittgenstein I have just mentioned is the philosopher Ludwig Wittgenstein (1889–1951) and not some other member of that large and distinguished family.

The early drafts of 'The Second Coming' mention Germans and Russia;[39] but when the poem was published these nationals and this nation were gone, and the poem, Terence Brown says, 'seemed to bear more on Irish affairs than on the general European crisis'.[40] But of course the poem was never *not* about Irish affairs, and this is where the question of reference needs some thought. We can go several ways on this matter. Paul Muldoon thinks, in so far as I understand his mischievous claim—he takes an implied but unmentioned cork from a wine bottle in the poem 'All Soul's Night' as a connection to the city of Cork, which in turn conjures up the Mayor of Cork, Terence Mac-Swiney, dying in a hunger-strike in Brixton Gaol—that Irish affairs are always present in Irish poems (but not presumably

[39] Jon Stallworthy, *Between the Lines* (Oxford: the Clarendon Press, 1963), 18–19.

[40] *The Life of W. B. Yeats,* 271.

more than French affairs are present in French poems).[41] Helen Vendler, on the other hand, writing about 'Nineteen Hundred and Nineteen', takes a series of steps away from Ireland. 'Irish events', she says, 'are not Yeats' principal focus.' It's true that 'the theme of the sequence' is 'murderous local and European bloodshed', but the underlying subject is 'the recurrent multiform and age-old violence of human beings.'[42] Seamus Deane, bringing us back to 'The Second Coming', and making me feel I was not entirely as wrong as I thought I was, asks, 'Can the bestial be born again as demonic? Can the mob be born again as a people, as a nation? That would truly be a second coming. It became known as fascism.'[43]

A poem can refer to history in more than one way, and to more than one history. I picture a poem in this respect as something like a dream in Freud's account of it: every element in the dream reflects more than one provocation in waking life; every waking anxiety finds more than one expression in the dream. This is not to say a poem can mean anything; only that a poem, like a dream, will reveal most to us when the patient and analyst are working together. One of our problems is that literary critics and scholars often have a version of what Wittgenstein called, in philosophy, a contempt for the particular case. Well, literary critics are generally too nice to feel contempt for the particular case. They feel sorry for it, they want to lend it a bit of the dignity that

---

[41] Paul Muldoon, *The End of the Poem* (New York: Farrar, Straus and Giroux, 2006), 26–7.

[42] *Our Secret Discipline*, 64, 75, 65.

[43] Quoted in *The Life of W. B. Yeats*, 272.

comes from belonging to a larger, even universal condition. This is how we leave local violence, or local anything, behind and fly to the vaster question. I think pretty much the opposite—that the local is always more interesting than the global—but of course I can't do without some kind of principle of generalization, and that thought itself is a generalized preference. My hope is that an exemplary case might retain enough particulars to avoid falling into sheer abstraction; that we may be able to see and describe the difference between particular, multiple meanings and any flattened out, single, larger meaning.

Think of the moment when the newly-remarried Gertrude, in *Hamlet*, invites her son to 'cast [his] nighted colour off' and no longer 'seek for [his] noble father in the dust:

> Thou know'st 'tis common; all that lives must die,
> Passing through nature to eternity.

Hamlet says, 'Ay, madam, it is common'. Death comes to us all and so do platitudes. How can her thought help Hamlet, when the question is not whether men die but whether widows should remain widows for such a short time. The (truthful) generality not only fails to address the specific case, it also transfers the argument from remarriage to mortality—unless of course Gertrude really hasn't understood what Hamlet is up to, and genuinely thinks a banality will console a grieving son.

Yeats' wonderful line 'Man is in love and loves what vanishes' works in much the same way. It is true, but would not be much of a consolation for the relatives of a person shot by the Black and Tans. There is a gap between the general truth of mortality and two quite different specificities: the specificity of any individual death and the specificity of every death that is not natural—in the second instance the time and place and manner of death become relevant as they are not in the case of natural death at a certain age. There is a similar gap between any historical event and the urge to compare it with other, insufficiently similar events and/or to fold it into a generalizable claim of meaning. We can cross the gap, and often have to; but the gap subsists beneath the crossing, and our greater or lesser awareness of the gap affects our passage.

With this proposition I arrive at a famous attempt to connect Irish affairs with a European crisis, namely Conor Cruise O'Brien's bid to link the Black and Tans to the Nazis. This remarkable essay is for most of its duration going in a different direction, since it offers a rebuke to all those readers of Yeats who like to get away from the particular case when the case is political. These readers obviously can't deny Yeats' involvement in politics, from the founding of the Abbey Theatre to his spell in the Irish senate, but they can suggest this person is not the 'true Yeats', because the true Yeats is a lyric poet, without history, just as Marina Tsvetaeva said such poets are. O'Brien amusingly divides these folks into three groups: 'those who are bored by Irish politics, those who are bored by all politics, and those who are frightened of Yeats politics'.[44] O'Brien insists that Yeats did far more than flirt with fascism, and that when he stopped his more than flirting it was not because he

---

[44] Conor Cruise O'Brien, 'Passion and Cunning', in *In Excited Reverie*, ed A. N. Jeffares and K. G. W. Cross (New York: Macmillan, 1965), 209.

had seen the liberal light but because he thought the movement was not going to work in Ireland. O'Brien accuses Yeats of writing 'Mussolini prose', and also, with great relish, reminds us (twice) of Yeats' admiration for the severity of Kevin O'Higgins as minister of the Free State. 'Seventy-seven executions did not repel him, on the contrary, they made him admire O'Higgins all the more.'[45] But then, O'Brien argues in a beautiful swerving movement, the poetry tells us a different story, or allows us to see a better story hiding in the prose. We could, he suggests, think of 'the political prose and the poetry ... as cognate expressions of a fundamental force, anterior to both politics and poetry'. This force would be 'Yeats' profound and tragic intuitive—and intelligent—awareness ... of what the First World War had set loose, of what was already moving towards Hitler and the Second World War'.[46] O'Brien knows what we are going to say.

It may be objected that 'Nineteen Hundred and Nineteen' and 'The Second Coming' were written not about the coming of Fascism but about the Anglo-Irish War and the Black and Tans. The distinction is not absolute: the Black and Tans were in fact an early manifestation of an outlook and methods which the Nazis were later to perfect.[47]

There are all kinds of things wrong with this line of thought, and I don't believe these poems are, even allowing for the

---

[45] 'Passion and Cunning', 247, 261.
[46] Ibid. 274–5.
[47] Ibid. 276.

shifting of reference, about the coming of fascism in any immediate sense—O'Brien's own argument suggests they are not,
since Yeats would have no reason to be as horrified as we are.
Of course the Nazis and the Black and Tans recruited a lot of
thugs, but you don't need 'an outlook and methods' for that,
still less a tragic awareness of what's wrong with the twentieth
century. Hitler and two world wars have turned into ciphers,
abstract markers of disaster, the way Auschwitz is often, rather
cruelly, used as shorthand for atrocity—even by someone as
careful as Adorno.

Still, I do believe O'Brien is on to something, and I believe it
is through Yeats, and in particular through 'Nineteen Hundred
and Nineteen', that he has got there. There can't be much mile-
age in the claim that the twentieth century is more violent than
any other. Think of the competition, and how would we quan-
tify such things anyway? Nor do I think we can really argue
that the twentieth century invented new forms of violence—
although it did invent several horrible new technologies, and
there would be a lot more to be said about this instance. But it
can be demonstrated, through Yeats and some other witnesses
I am going to call in a moment, that certain writers in the
early twentieth century had just such an awareness as O'Brien
evokes, and that they intuited something more precise than a
general moral disaster. When Yeats says, in another famous line
from 'The Second Coming', that 'mere anarchy is loosed upon
the world', he does not mean mere disorder. He means what is
perceived as a new degree of uncontrollable violence and a new
realm of impunity.

V

Both Yeats and Walter Benjamin invoke the story of Niobe in this context. Niobe was the Queen of Thebes who boasted of having so many children, and in particular of having more children than the goddess Leto, who had only two. They were both gods—Apollo and Artemis—but she didn't feel this entirely made up for the lack of numbers, and sent them off to wipe out Niobe's entire brood. Niobe herself turned to stone out of grief—a stone that nevertheless kept on weeping.

For Yeats Niobe is an image of civilization on the edge of ending.

A civilization is a struggle to keep self-control, and in this is like some great tragic person, some Niobe who must display an almost superhuman will or the cry will not touch our sympathy. The loss of control over thought comes towards the end; first a sinking in upon the moral being, then the last surrender, the irrational cry, revelation—the scream of Juno's peacock.[48]

'Nineteen Hundred and Nineteen' offers first a mirror image of this story, the picture of a civilization which had delusions at the end instead of superhuman will, and which can only arouse our fury not our sympathy; and then the poem offers a direct representation, a portrait of the last surrender, the irrational cry, and the ambiguous revelation of the lurching spirit. Juno's peacock has become Lady Kyteler's peacock feathers.

[48] W. B. Yeats, *A Vision (1938)* (New York: Macmillan, 1961), 268.

Benjamin's essay 'On the Critique of Violence' was written and published in 1921, and very much belongs to the world of the mentalities I am describing—although it is often taken as if it were a timeless bit of philosophizing.[49] Benjamin distinguishes between 'mythic violence' and 'divine violence', Greek and Jewish respectively, where the first is 'pernicious' because its only purpose is to establish power and keep it in place, and the second is calamitous but 'pure, immediate' in its action.[50] Jehovah annihilating a whole company of his people compares favourably to the Greek gods leaving Niobe to suffer. Mythic violence is 'fundamentally identical with legal violence', the violence associated with legality itself, *Rechtmäßigkeit*. Divine violence, whatever its costs, has to do with justice, *Gerechtigkeit*, and revolution would be its 'highest' human expression. I should insist that Benjamin says all kinds of human matters can be treated without violence, through trust and understanding and other moderate exchanges, through what Jacques Derrida, glossing this passage, calls 'the culture of the heart'.[51] But Benjamin doesn't appear to believe that either politics or theology can do without violence.

[49] Agamben doesn't treat it as timeless but he does want to extend its time. 'Benjamin's "Critique of Violence" proves the necessary, and even today, indispensable premise of every inquiry into sovereignty'. *Homo Sacer*, 63.

[50] Walter Benjamin, 'Critique of Violence', in *Selected Writings*, vol 1, trans. Edmund Jephcott (Cambridge, Mass.: Harvard University Press, 1996), 252.

[51] Jacques Derrida, 'Force of Law', in *Acts of Religion*, trans. Mary Quaintance (New York and London: Routledge, 2002), 284.

For him, Niobe is a person whose 'arrogance calls down fate upon her not because her arrogance offends against the law but because it challenges fate ... Violence therefore bursts upon Niobe from the uncertain, ambiguous sphere of fate'. This is because violence for the gods is 'not a means to their ends, scarcely a manifestation of their will, but primarily a manifestation of their existence'.[52] In this view the Greek gods themselves, for whose collective, unstoppable incoherence fate appears to be another name, are something like an ancient, immortal version of Yeats' drunken soldiers; and it can scarcely be an accident that they emerge in this light in 1921. By contrast, Jehovah's justice, instanced in his destruction of the Levites of the company of Korah is lethal but intelligible.[53] I am far from understanding this argument very well, but it does seem clear that such a view of the Jewish God, in Berlin in the early days of the Weimar Republic, makes sense most immediately as a back-formation from the horror of the vision of the Greeks I have just described; the intellectual shock-effect of the perceived prevalence of random violence, of the sense that even legal violence feels random because it serves not justice for persons but the impersonal legitimacy of the tyrannous state. Of course it may be that Jehoavah is in trouble too. In a brilliantly perverse reading of this passage

---

[52] 'Critique of Violence', 248.
[53] 'And the Lord spake unto Moses and unto Aaron, saying, Separate yourselves from among this congregation, that I may consume them in a moment ... And the earth opened her mouth, and swallowed them up, and their houses, and all the men that appertained unto Korah, and all their houses.' *Numbers* 16, 20–1, 32.

Zizek suggests, providing his own italics, that 'divine violence is *a sign of God's … own impotence*'.[54]

Here is another instance from the same time and culture: Augsburg, 1919. This is the poem by Brecht called 'The Song of the Soldier of the Red Army'. There is a slight mystery about this poem, since Brecht performed it in a tavern when he wrote it, and afterwards, in 1927, published it in a volume. Then he refused to allow it to be reprinted at all, and it vanished from view until after his death. A friend of Brecht's says this is because the poet was concerned, conveniently for my argument, about the uncertainty of reference in the poem: people might think it was about the Russian Red Army when it was really about the short-lived Bavarian Red Army, or vice-versa. This is worth worrying about, since the difference makes a difference, and even if we thought the poem might refer to both armies, we wouldn't want to blur the distinction between them, as if all Red Armies were alike—once you've seen one you've seen them all. Still, none of this seems to offer grounds for disowning the poem, and I am going to suggest that Brecht, who could put up with all kinds of unpleasantness, much of it caused by himself, felt he had come too close in spirit to the kind of uninformed, unappeased, sardonic anger that, among many other things, fed into Nazism. As Benjamin had come too close, in Derrida's reading, to the high intellectual justification for divine violence that might also have been that of some of the thinkers of the Third Reich.[55]

---

[54] Slavoj Zizek, *Violence* (London: Profile Books, 2008), 170.
[55] 'When one thinks of the gas chambers and the cremation ovens, [Benjamin's] allusion to an extermination that would be expiatory because

Brecht's poem has ten stanzas, quatrains; here are the last six:

> In rain and in the murky wind
> Hard stone seems good to sleep upon.
> The rain washed out our filthy eyes and cleansed them
> Of filth and many a various sin.

> Often at night the sky turned red
> They thought red dawn had come again.
> That was a fire, but the dawn came also.
> Freedom, my children, never came.

> And so, wherever they might be
> They looked around and said, it's hell.
> The time went by. The latest hell, though,
> Was never the very last hell of all.

> So many hells were still to come.
> Freedom, my children, never came.
> The time goes by. But if the heavens came now
> These heavens would be much the same.

> When once our body's eaten up
> With an exhausted heart in it
> The army spews our skin and bones out
> Into cold and shallow pits.

> And with our body hard from rain
> And with our hearts all scarred by ice

bloodless must cause one to shudder'. 'Force of Law', 298. Giorgio Agamben says this reading represents 'a peculiar misunderstanding' of Benjamin's thought. *Homo Sacer*, trans. Daniel Heller-Roazen (Stanford: Stanford University Press, 1998), 64.

> And with our bloodstained empty hands we
> Come grinning into your paradise.[56]

It's the last turn that alters everything, and gives the poem the sudden feel of a revelation. The soldiers are cold and tired and complaining. They have lost hope and they have blood-stained hands: they are soldiers. They die, and they tell us about dying. Then all at once they are grinning and saved. Well, they have arrived in paradise. No, in our paradise, the paradise of right or left, the rescued bourgeois world or the new order after the revolution, neither of which would have been glad to see the dirty soldiers of the earlier conflict again. That's why the soldiers are grinning. They know how upset we are to see them. And they seem at the end to know who they are. They are not the drunken soldiery of 'Nineteen Hundred and Nineteen'—I am, as I said, trying to hang on to specifics as well as make comparisons—but they are violent dead men who won't die, who have been through several secular hells, and their grins promise all kinds of havoc in the place we thought was perfect. They are not 'the worst rogues and rascals' of Yeats' poem; they are not even 'weasels fighting in a hole'. They have been fighting in a hole, but they are not weasels. But they are anarchic enough, convincing enough, lively enough, to end any dream of order. We just can't tell what they will do when they stop grinning.

Here's a last witness for the sense that a new, unfocused form of violence is on the march. There is a very nice academic and historical touch here, since if you turn to the acknowledgements

[56] Bertolt Brecht, 'Song of the Soldier of the Red Army', in *Poems*, trans. John Willett (London: Methuen, 1976), 23.

page of the translation of Blok's poem *The Twelve* by Jon Stallworthy and Peter France, you will find an expression of gratitude to Sir Maurice Bowra 'who in a tutorial on Yeats's poetry introduced the unknown name of Alexander Blok'.[57] Bowra had made the connection long ago, and we meet yet another set of soldiers out of control.

In *The Twelve*, a poem of twelve sections written in January 1918—as you see, we're not travelling very far in time—we encounter the Red Guard, rattling through the streets of St Petersburg. The night is dark and windy, there is snow everywhere, passing pedestrians slip and fall, a banner hangs across the street: 'Full power to the Constituent Assembly'. An old lady wonders what it means and thinks the cloth could be better used for keeping children warm. The soldiers are singing, they catch sight of, and sneer at, a writer, a priest. The local prostitutes hold their own constituent assembly, and decide on a new set of prices. The first, long section ends:

> Black sky grows blacker.
>
> Anger, sorrowful anger
> seethes in the breast ...
> Black anger, holy anger ...
>
> Friend!
> Keep your eyes skinned![58]

---

[57] Alexander Blok, *The Twelve and Other Poems*, trans. Jon Stallworthy and Peter France (New York: Oxford University Press, 1970), acknowledgements page.

[58] Ibid., 144.

In the next sections, a single soldier takes the lead in the song. He sees his old girlfriend Katya with a new man, Vanya, a former comrade who seems to have gone over to the other side. It's a good life, the Red Guards think, their battle against the unsleeping bourgeois enemy, they're going to 'light a fire through all the world'—and deal with Katya and Vanya as well. The single soldier recalls his earlier acts of violence, which he seems to think of as a kind of sexual discipline—

> Across your collar-bone, my Katya,
> a knife has scarred the flesh;
> and there below your bosom, Katya,
> that little scratch is fresh …
>
> Do you remember that officer—
> the knife put an end to him.[59]

Then suddenly there's shooting, Vanya is running and Katya is dead. Our soldier—'the poor killer', as the poem calls him, 'the poor murderer' in another translation—gloats and then feels sorry for himself, sentimental as only a thug can be. But his friends cheer him up and he gets back in the marching, shouting mood.

> What the hell!
> It's not a sin to have some fun!
> Abusing God's name as they go,
> all twelve march onward into snow …
> prepared for anything,
> regretting nothing …

---

[59] *The Twelve and Other Poems*, 149.

> Their rifles at the ready
> for the unseen enemy.[60]

The soldiers 'march with sovereign tread', but they are getting nervous and shoot at shadows. And then all at once …

At the end of *The Twelve*, after the shooting and in the dark streets, the guards see something in front of them, Blok's version of what happens when a world ends. He said that when he was writing the poem and for several days after he had finished it he heard a noise all around him—'probably that of the crumbling of the old world', were his words. Here are the last lines of the poem:

> So they march with sovereign tread …
> Behind them limps the hungry dog,
> and wrapped in wild snow at their head
> carrying a blood-red flag—
> soft-footed where the blizzard swirls,
> invulnerable where bullets crossed—
> crowned with a crown of snowflake pearls,
> a flowery diadem of frost,
> ahead of them goes Jesus Christ.[61]

These soldiers of course are not quite those of Brecht and not quite those of Yeats; cousins rather than closer relatives. And the soldier has his reason for killing Katya. A stupid, ugly and inadequate reason, to be sure, but enough to acquit him of the charge of mindlessness. As Tom Paulin says in another poem in

---

[60] Ibid. 153, 157.
[61] Ibid., 160.

The Invasion Handbook, 'Contrary as it appears to all received opinion, Hitler had a mind. It was coarse, turbid, narrow, rigid, cruel, but it was a mind.'[62] The violence in question, the kind intuited by Yeats and half-identified by Conor Cruise O'Brien, is not always groundless; it may have grounds, even if they are fantasmatic and displaced. But it hovers between plan and accident, like reprisals, like a drive-by shooting by the Black and Tans, like the death of Lorca, and in every case the distance from what might look like an immediate or sufficient reason is considerable. Such violence always feels random and it does usually go unpunished. It feels like an incarnation of meaninglessness; it feels like an uncontrollable mystery.

But the most startling effect of Blok's ending, of course, is its literalization of the second coming, its version of the sphinx or Robert Artisson. Here there is no rough beast, no slouching towards Bethlehem, and no lurching spirit from old Kilkenny either. No terminal question mark, as in 'The Second Coming', no doubt about what or who will appear when the hour comes round at last. The true successor to Jesus Christ, the victim and master of Calvary's turbulence, is ... Jesus Christ. Blok said all kinds of confusing things about Christ's likely sympathy with the Revolution—'a simple matter for anyone who has read the Gospels and thought about them', he claimed[63]—but they scarcely tame the poem's terror. Christ seems to have been conjured up by the weather and the Revolution and the raw energy of the Red Guards. 'Their only good quality, if it is one', Stallworthy and France say, 'is their

---

[62] *The Invasion Handbook*, 31.
[63] *The Twelve and Other Poems*, 34.

determination to march on through the blizzard and the night, disregarding purely personal tragedies ... which must be left behind with the rest of the old world'.[64] Except that the 'purely personal' can no longer exist in such a storm, not even to be left behind. Katya's murder, that not quite groundless but nevertheless random-seeming event, is an essential part of the poem's final vision, a memorandum of its recklessly paid price. Christ must know better than anyone when a world is dying, and he who remembers the fall of every sparrow could hardly forget a pointless human death. And yet he leads the soldiers, he carries a blood-red flag, he is the ultimate, militant instance of what cannot be controlled: a Nietzschean Christ, let's say, ready to deny everything he preached in the Sermon on the Mount. Blok, like Yeats, like Benjamin, like Brecht, has found an image that answers to what is felt as a new disorder, the condition of a world that can only think of its ending, and can picture that ending only as a violent and desperate imitation of a promise.

I don't think we can say that literature resists history here, to return to Roland Barthes' ordinarily very useful formulation. Literature is miming history, singing along, humming history's scary tune. But that very singing, when done in this way, by these writers, offers the possibility of a critique, the glimpse of a future understanding. This is a future understanding in two senses. We haven't got it yet, and we are not yet looking at the horrors of the twentieth century O'Brien ascribes to Yeats' intuition; only at Russia and Germany and Ireland around 1920; only at pieces of the ground where those horrors grew, and where they perhaps had to grow.

[64] Ibid. 33.

FURTHER READING

Agamben, Giorgio. *Homo Sacer*, trans. Daniel Heller-Roazen. Stanford: Stanford University Press, 1998.

—— *The End of the Poem*, trans. Daniel Heller-Roazen. Stanford, Calif.: Stanford University Press, 1999.

Allison, Jonathan, ed. *Yeats' Political Identities*. Ann Arbor: University of Michigan Press, 1996.

Arendt, Hannah. *On Violence*. New York: Harcourt Brace, 1970.

Attridge, Derek. *The Rhythms of English Poetry*. London: Longman, 1982.

—— *Poetic Rhythm*. Cambridge: Cambridge University Press, 1995.

Auden, W. H. *Prose, Volume III (1949–1955)*. Princeton: Princeton University Press, 2007.

Barthes, Roland. *Sur Racine*. Paris: Seuil, 1963.

—— *S/Z*. Paris: Seuil, 1970.

—— *The Grain of the Voice*, trans. Linda Coverdale. London: Jonathan Cape, 1985.

—— *Mythologies*, trans. Annette Lavers. New York: Hill and Wang, 1994.

Beckett, J. C. *The Anglo-Irish Tradition*. Ithaca: Cornell University Press, 1976.

Bell, Michael. *Literature, Modernism and Myth*. Cambridge: Cambridge University Press, 1997.

—— *Sentimentalism, Ethics and the Culture of Feeling*. Basingstoke: Palgrave, 2000.

Benjamin, Walter. *Selected Writings* vol. 1, ed. Marcus Bullock and Michael W. Jennings. Cambridge, Mass.: Harvard University Press, 1996.

Bew, Paul. *Ireland: The Politics of Enmity, 1789–2006*. Oxford: Oxford University Press, 2007.

Blackmur, R. P. *Selected Essays*, ed. Denis Donoghue. New York: Ecco Press, 1985.

Blok, Alexander. *The Twelve and Other Poems*, translated by Jon Stallworthy and Peter France. New York: Oxford University Press, 1970.

Boland, Eavan. *In a Time of Violence*. Manchester: Carcanet, 1994.

—— *Object Lessons*. New York and London: Norton, 1995.

—— *Domestic Violence*. Manchester: Carcanet Press, 1999.

Brecht, Bertolt. *Poems,* various translators. London: Methuen, 1976.

Brogan, T. V. F. *English Versification*. Baltimore: Johns Hopkins University Press, 1981.

Bromwich, David. *Skeptical Music*. Chicago and London: Chicago University Press, 2001.

Brown, Terence. *The Life of W. B. Yeats*. Oxford: Blackwell, 2001.

Campbell, Fergus. *Land and Revolution: Nationalist Politics in the West of Ireland 1891–1921*. Oxford: Oxford University Press, 2005.

Carey, John (ed). *Andrew Marvell*. Harmondsworth: Penguin, 1969.

Carson, Ciaran. *The Twelfth of Never*. London: Picador, 1999.

Croft, Barbara L. *Stylistic Arrangements*. Lewisburg: Bucknell University Press, 1987.

Cullingford, Elizabeth. *Yeats, Ireland, and Fascism*. London: Macmillan, 1981.

Dangerfield, George. *The Strange Death of Liberal England*. London: MacGibbon and Kee, 1966.

Dennett, Daniel. *Consciousness Explained*. New York: Little, Brown, 1991.

Derrida, Jacques. *La dissémination*. Paris: Seuil, 1972.

——*Acts of Religion*, various translators. New York and London: Routledge, 2002.

Doggett, Rob. *Deep-rooted Things: Empire and Nation in the Poetry and Drama of W. B. Yeats*. Notre Dame: Notre Dame University Press, 2006.

Donoghue, Denis. *W. B. Yeats*. New York: Viking, 1971.

——'Yeats: The New Political Issue', *Princeton University Library Chronicle* (Spring 1998).

——*Adam's Curse: Reflections on Religion and Literature*. Notre Dame: University of Notre Dame Press, 2001.

Dupee, F. W. *Henry James*. New York: Delta, 1965.

Edwards, Ruth Dudley. *Patrick Pearse: the Triumph of Failure*. Dublin and Portland, Oregon: Irish Academic Press, 2006.

Eliot, T. S. *Selected Prose*, ed. Frank Kermode. New York: Harcourt, Brace, Jovanovich, 1975.

Faulkner, Peter. *Yeats: The Tower and The Winding Stair*. Milton Keynes: Open University Press, 1987.

Foster, R. F. *Modern Ireland 1600–1972*. London: Penguin, 1989, c1988.

——*W. B. Yeats: A Life I: The Apprentice Mage*. Oxford: Oxford University Press, 1997.

——*W. B. Yeats: A Life II. The Arch-Poet*. Oxford: Oxford University Press, 2003.

——*Luck and the Irish: A Brief History of Change from 1970*. Oxford: Oxford University Press, 2008.

Garvin, Tom. *1922: The Birth of Irish Democracy*. Dublin: Gill and Macmillan, 1996.

Gordon, Lyndall. *A Private Life of Henry James*. New York and London: W. W. Norton, 1998.

Grene, Nicholas. 'Yeats and Dates', in Nicholas Allen and Eve Patten (eds.), *That Island Never Found*. Dublin and Portland: Four Courts Press, 2007.

Gregory, Lady Augusta. *Journals*, vol 1. New York: Oxford University Press, 1978.

Harper, George Mills. *The Making of Yeats's A Vision*. New York: Macmillan, 1987.

Heaney, Seamus. *North*. London: Faber, 1975.

—— *Selected Poems 1965–1975*. London: Faber, 1980.

—— *Finders Keepers*. New York: Farrar, Straus Giroux, 2002.

Hobbes, Thomas. *Leviathan*. London: Penguin, 1985.

Hough, Graham. *The Mystery Religion of W. B. Yeats*. Brighton: Harvester, 1984.

Howes, Marjorie. *Yeats's Nations: Gender, Class and Irishness*. Cambridge: Cambridge University Press, 1996.

Howes, Marjorie and John Kelly eds. *The Cambridge Companion to W. B. Yeats*. Cambridge: Cambridge University Press, 2006.

Jakobson, Roman. *Questions de poétique*, various translators. Paris: Editions du Seuil, 1973.

James, Henry. *The Art of the Novel*. New York: Scribner's, 1962.

—— *Literary Criticism*. New York: Library of America, 1984.

—— *Letters, Volume IV*. Cambridge, Mass: Harvard University Press, 1984.

Jeffares, A. N. and A. S. Knowland, *A Commentary on the Collected Plays of W. B. Yeats*. Stanford: Stanford University Press, 1975.

Jeffares, A. N. *A New Commentary on the Poems of W. B. Yeats*. Stanford: Stanford University Press, 1984.

Kee, Robert. *The Green Flag, Volume Three: Ourselves Alone*. London: Quartet Books, 1976.

Kelly, John. *A W. B. Yeats Chronology*. London: Palgrave, 2003.

Kermode, Frank. *Romantic Image*. New York: Vintage, 1964.

——'The Anglo-Irish Hyphen', *The Hopkins Review*, NS 1.1 (Winter 2008).

Kiberd, Declan. *Inventing Ireland*. London: Jonathan Cape, 1995.

——*Irish Classics*. London: Granta Books, 2000.

Leighton, Angela. *On Form*. Oxford: Oxford University Press, 2007.

Lévi-Strauss, Claude. *Anthropologie structurale*. Paris: Plon, 1955.

Longenbach, James. *Stone Cottage: Pound, Yeats and Modernism*. Oxford: Oxford University Press, 1988.

——*The Art of the Poetic Line*. Saint Paul, Minn.: Graywolf Press, 2008.

Lloyd, David. *Anomalous States*. Dublin: the Lilliput Press, 1993.

——'Rage against the Divine', *South Atlantic Quarterly*, 106:2 (Spring 2007).

——*Irish Times*. Dublin: Field Day, 2008.

Loewenstein, David. *Representing Revolution in Milton and his Contemporaries*. Cambridge: Cambridge University Press, 2001.

Lyons, F. S. *Culture and Anarchy in Ireland 1890–1939*. Oxford: Clarendon Press, 1979.

Marvell, Andrew. *Complete Poetry*, ed. George deF. Lord. London: J. M. Dent, 1984.

——*The Poems*, ed. Nigel Smith. London: Pearson and Longman, 2003.

Mayer, Arno. *The Furies*. Princeton: Princeton University Press, 2000.

McCormack, W. J. *From Burke to Beckett*. Cork: Cork University Press, 1994.

——*Blood Kindred: W. B. Yeats, the Life the Death, the Politics*. London: Pimlico, 2005.

Miller, J. Hillis. *Poets of Reality*. Oxford: Oxford University Press, 1966.

—— *The Linguistic Moment*. Princeton: Princeton University Press, 1985.

Muldoon, Paul. *Selected Poems 1968–1986*. Farrar, Straus and Giroux, 1993.

—— *To Ireland, I*. Oxford: Oxford University Press, 2000.

—— *Moy Sand and Gravel*. New York: Farrar, Straus and Giroux, 2002.

—— *Horse Latitudes*. New York: Farrar, Straus and Giroux, 2006.

—— *The End of the Poem*. New York: Farrar Straus and Giroux, 2006.

North, Michael. *The Political Aesthetic of Yeats, Eliot, and Pound*. Cambridge: Cambridge University Press, 1991.

O'Brien, Conor Cruise. 'Passion and Cunning', in *In Excited Reverie*, ed. A. N. Jeffares and K. G. W. Cross. New York: Macmillan, 1965.

Owen, Alex. *The Place of Enchantment*. Chicago: University of Chicago Press, 2004.

Parrish, Stephen Maxfield (ed). *A Concordance to the Poems of W. B. Yeats*. Ithaca and London: Cornell University Press, 1963.

Patterson, Annabel. *Marvell and the Civic Crown*. Princeton: Princeton University Press, 1978.

Paulin, Tom. *The Invasion Handbook*. London: Faber and Faber, 2002.

—— *The Camouflage School*. Thame: The Clutag Press, 2007.

Plato. *Phaedrus*, trans. W. C. Helmbold and W. G. Rabinowitz. Indianapolis: Bobbs-Merrill, 1956.

Ragussis, Michael. *The Subterfuge of Art*. Baltimore: Johns Hopkins University Press, 1978.

Ramazani, Jahan. *Yeats and the Poetry of Death*. New Haven: Yale University Press, 1990.

Saddlemyer, Ann. *Becoming George*. Oxford: Oxford University Press, 2002.

Said, E. W. *Culture and Imperialism*. New York: Knopf, 1993.

Snodgrass, W. D. 'The Use of Meter', *The Southern Review* (1999).

Stallworthy, Jon. *Between the Lines*. Oxford: the Clarendon Press, 1963.

Stern, J. P. *The Dear Purchase*. Cambridge: Cambridge University Press, 1995.

Stevens, Wallace. *Letters*. New York: Knopf, 1966.

Symons, Arthur. *Images of Good and Evil*. Poole and New York: Woodstock Books, 1996.

Taylor, Richard. *A Reader's Guide to the Plays of W. B. Yeats*. New York: St Martin's Press, 1984.

Thompson, John. *The Founding of English Metre*. New York: Columbia University Press, 1961.

Toliver, Harold. *Marvell's Ironic Vision*. New Haven and London: Yale University Press, 1965).

Townshend, Charles. *Political Violence in Ireland*. Oxford: Clarendon Press, 1983.

——*Ireland: the 20ᵗʰ Century*. London: Arnold, 1999.

——*Easter 1916: the Irish Rebellion*. London: Penguin, 2006.

Trilling, Lionel. *The Liberal Imagination*. New York: New York Review of Books Classics, 2008.

Tsvetaeva, Marina. *Art in the Light of Conscience*, trans. Angela Livingstone. Cambridge, Mass.: Harvard University Press, 1992.

Vendler, Helen. *Yeats's Vision and the Later Plays*. Cambridge, Mass.: Harvard University Press, 1963.

——*Poets Thinking*. Cambridge, Mass.: Harvard University Press, 2004.

—— *Our Secret Discipline: Yeats and Lyric Form*. Cambridge: Harvard University Press, 2007.

Weber, Max. *Politik als Beruf.* Munich and Leipzig: Duneker and Humblot, 1926.

Wheatcroft, Geoffrey. 'Conor Cruise O'Brien', *New York Review of Books*, 26 March 2009.

Whitaker, Thomas R. *Swan and Shadow: Yeats's Dialogue with History*. Washington, D. C.: Catholic University of America Press, 1989.

Williams, Raymond. *Keywords*. London: Fontana, 1976.

Wimsatt, W. K. Jr., and Monroe C. Beardsley, *The Verbal Icon: Studies in the Meaning of Poetry*. Lexington: University of Kentucky Press, 1954.

Wittgenstein, Ludwig. *Tractatus Logico-Philosophicus*, trans. C. K. Ogden. London: Routledge, 1999.

Wolfson, Susan. *Formal Charges*. Stanford, Calif.: Stanford University Press, 1997.

Yeats, W. B. *The Variorum Edition of the Poems*, ed. Peter Allt and Russell K. Alspach. New York: Macmillan, 1957.

—— *A Vision (1938)*. New York: Macmillan, 1961.

—— *Essays and Introductions*. New York: Macmillan, 1968.

—— *Collected Plays*. London and Basingstoke: Macmillan, 1982.

—— *Yeats's Vision Papers*, ed. Steve L. Adams, Barbara J. Frieling, and Sandra L. Sprayberry. Iowa City: Iowa University Press, 1992.

—— *The Collected Poems,* ed. Richard J Finneran. New York: Scribner, 1996.

—— *Autobiographies*. New York: Scribner, 1999.

—— (ed). *A Book of Irish Verse*. London and New York: Routledge, 2002.

—— *The Tower: A Facsimile Edition*. New York: Scribner, 2004.

Yeats, W. B. *The Tower*, ed. Richard J Finneran, with Jared Curtis and Ann Saddlemyer. Ithaca: Cornell University Press, 2007.

——*A Vision: The Original 1925 Version*, ed. Catherine E. Paul and Margaret Mills Harper. New York: Scribner, 2008.

Zizek, Slavoj. *Violence*. London: Profile Books, 2008.

INDEX

Adams, Henry 94
Addison, Joseph 101
Adorno, T. W. 21
A. E. (George Russell) 33
Agamben, Giorgio 15, 117, 118, 121, 133
Akhmatova, Anna 185
'All Souls' Night' 74–8, 100, 127, 129, 211
'Among School Children' 49
Andrewes, Lancelot 10
Apocalypse Now 141
Ardagh, Bishop of 23
Arendt, Hannah 16, 17, 137, 143, 144, 149
Attridge, Derek 91, 93, 122, 128, 130
Auden, W. H. 127, 137, 188, 189

Balzac, Honoré de 1
Barthes, Roland 1, 18, 139, 184, 227
Baudelaire, Charles 70
Beardsley, Monroe 96, 98
'Beautiful Speech' 180
Beckett, Samuel 138
Bell, Michael 143
Benjamin, Walter 16, 19, 152, 217, 218, 220, 227
Blackmur, R. P. B. 93, 94, 100, 137
Blake, William 12, 64, 79, 101
Blok, Alexander 186, 187, 223, 225, 226, 227
Boland, Eavan 141, 142, 179, 180, 181, 182

Book of the Homeless 46
Book of Common Prayer 198
Borges, Jorge Luis 96, 97, 98
Bowles, Jane 189
Bowles, Paul 189
Bowra, Maurice 223
Bradley, F. H. 84
Brancusi, Constantin 85
Brecht, Bertolt 220, 221, 225, 227
Bridges, Robert 128
Britten, Benjamin 189
Bromwich, David 143
Broughton, Rhoda 163
Brueghel, Pieter 101
Brooks, Cleanth 91, 146, 147, 150, 151, 152
Brown, Terence 31, 194, 210, 211
Bush, Douglas 147, 150, 151
Byron, George Gordon 112

Cabinet of Dr Caligari, The 33
Calvary 64
Campbell, Fergus 22, 28
Carson, Ciaran 191
Cathleen ni Houlihan 188, 191–4, 197
Chamberlain, Arthur Neville 210
Charles I 144, 147
'Choice, The' 108
'Cimetière marin, Le' 82
Claudel, Paul 197
Coleridge, S. T. 90

Connolly, James 195, 196
Conrad, Joseph 45, 70
Constantius 141
Coppola, Francis Ford 141
Croft, Barbara L. 61–2
Cromwell, Oliver 144, 145, 147, 150, 151, 152, 153, 154, 155, 156, 182
'Curse of Cromwell, The' 153–6

'Dance of the Daughters of Herodias, The' 205
Dangerfield, George 43, 162, 163, 164, 165, 166
Davis, Thomas 151
Deane, Seamus 212
Dear Purchase, The 197
Derrida, Jacques 218, 220
de Valera, Eamon 33
Dial, The 30, 37
Domestic Violence 179
Don Juan 112
Donoghue, Denis 9, 188
'Double Vision of Michael Robartes, The' 109
Dr Faustus 198

'Easter 1916' 12, 42, 91, 199
Edwards, Betham 164
Einstein, Albert 78
Eliot, T. S. 10, 90, 166, 167, 168
'End of the Poem, The' 117

Faerie Queene, The 51
Fairfax, Thomas 144
Farr, Florence 76
Flaubert, Gustave 204
Ford, Ford Madox 44, 45, 47
Foster, R. W. 7, 28, 31, 33, 43, 154, 196
France, Peter 223

Frankfurt, Harry 169
Freud, Sigmund 33, 142, 212
Frost, Robert 128
Fuller, Loie 3, 49, 50, 51

Galway Observer, The 28
García Lorca, Federico 190, 191, 226
'Gift of Harun El-Rashid, The' 63
Gibbon, Edward 141
Gladstone, William Ewart 140
Goethe, Johann Wolfgang von 184, 185, 187
Gonne, Maude 67
Good Soldier, The 44–5
Gregory, Lady Augusta 20, 21, 28, 43, 55, 57, 188
Gregory, Margaret 22
Gregory, Robert 22, 24, 25, 27
Grene, Nicholas 30, 31
Gwynn, Stephen 188
Gypsy Ballads 191
'Gyres, The' 104

Hamlet 96, 213
Harper, George Mills 61, 64
Heaney, Seamus 94, 142, 178
Heine, Thomas Theodor 50
Heraclitus 79
'High Talk' 111
Hitler, Adolf 210, 215, 216, 226
Hobbes, Thomas 148, 169
Homer 146
Homo Sacer 15
Hopkins, G. M. 63
Horace 35
'Horatian Ode, An' 142, 143, 168
Horse Latitudes 169
Horton, William Thomas 76
Hough, Graham 14

'Hour before Dawn, An' 111
'Hugh Selwyn Mauberley' 44
Hume, David 32

In a Time of Violence 179
'In Memory of Robert Gregory' 6
Invasion Handbook, The 187, 226

Jakobson, Roman 88
James, Henry 5, 35, 43, 44, 45, 46,
    163, 164, 165, 166, 181, 199, 202
Jeffares, A. N. 11, 38, 204
Johnson, Paul 162, 163
Jonson, Ben 157
Joyce, James 44

Kafka, Franz 96
Keats, John 64
Kermode, Frank 6, 50, 134
Knight, G. Wilson 68
Kyteler, Alice 136, 207, 208, 209,
    217

'Lamentation of the Old Pensioner,
    The' 108, 111
Landor, W. S. 58
'Lapis Lazuli' 36, 108
Larkin, Philip 97, 98
La Rochefoucauld, François de 101
Laws 144
Lee, Gypsy Rose 189
Leighton, Angela 30, 90, 128
Lenin, V. I. 156
Leviathan 148
Lévi-Strauss, Claude 2
Lewis, Percy Wyndham 85
Liebknecht, Karl 33
Lloyd, David 15, 19, 24
Loewenstein, David 150, 152
London Mercury, The 30

Longenbach, James 117, 128
Lord Jim 70
Lumière, Auguste 50
Lumière, Louis 50
Luther, Martin 198
Luxemburg, Rosa 33
Lyons, F. S. L. 195, 197

MacNeice, Louis 188, 191
MacSwiney, Terence 211
Maddox, Brenda 81
'Magi, The' 10–13
'Magic' 82
Mallarmé, Stéphane 70, 204
'Man and the Echo, The' 188
Mandestam, Osip 185
Mann, Thomas 197, 198
Marvell, Andrew 142, 143, 144, 145,
    146, 147, 148, 149, 150, 151, 152,
    153, 154, 168
Mathers, McGregor 76, 77
McCullers, Carson 189
McDiarmid, Lucy 28
'Meditations in Time of Civil
    War' 8, 92, 100, 108, 100
'Meru' 92, 106, 107, 108, 109
Milton, John 128
Muldoon, Paul 112, 127, 129, 142,
    169, 174, 175, 179, 188, 190,
    191, 211
Mussolini, Benito 59, 210

Nietzsche, Friedrich 58

O'Brien, Conor Cruise 196, 214,
    215, 216, 226, 227
Oedipus at Colonus 41
O'Higgins, Kevin 215
'Old Country, The' 169–75
On Form 30

Only Jealousy of Emer, The 64
'On the Critique of Violence' 218–20
Our Secret Discipline 88
Ovid 35

Paradise Lost 128
Pasternak, Boris 185
Patterson, Annabel 149
Paulin, Tom 142, 179, 187, 225
Pearse, Patrick 194, 195, 196, 197
Pettit, Philip 18
Phaedrus 96
Phidias 99
Plato 54, 144
Poetry 10
Poets Thinking 89
'Poets with History and Poets without History' 184
Pope, Alexander 90, 91
Pound, Ezra 7, 44, 46, 58, 127
'Prayer for My Daughter, A' 109
Pushkin, Alexander 184, 187

Quinn, Ellen or Eileen 22, 24, 28, 31, 191
Quinn John 46
Quinn, Malachi 20, 21

Ramazani, Jahan 132
'Reprisals' 24–7
Ragussis, Michael 36, 138
Responsibilities 10, 190
Rilke, Rainer Maria 29

'Sailing to Byzantium' 206
'Saint and the Hunchback, The' 111
Salgado, Gamini 97, 98
Sarrasine 1
Schwartz, Delmore 190

'Second Coming, The' 14, 78, 104, 202, 209, 210, 211, 212, 215, 216, 226
Shakespear, Olivia 55, 57
Shakespeare, William 35, 88, 89, 96, 108
Shelley, P. B. 64, 70, 101
Smith, Nigel 144
Snodgrass, W. D. 127
Socrates 96
'Song of the Soldier of the Red Army, The' 220–2
Spenser, Edmund 51, 151
Stallworthy, Jon 223
'Statues, The' 93
Steele, Richard 101
Stendhal 167
Stern, J. P. 197, 198
Stevens, Wallace 19
Stewart, Susan 134
Strange Death of Liberal England, The 162
Sturgis, Howard 163
Summers, Montague 204
Swift, Jonathan 101
Symons, Arthur 205
S/Z 1

Taylor, Richard 193
'Tell' 175–8
Tell, William 175, 177, 179
Thompson, John 117, 128
'Thoughts After Lambeth' 166
'Three Monuments' 111
'Time and Violence' 181
Toliver, Harold 150
Tone, Theobald Wolfe 195
'Towards Break of Day' 79
Tower, The (volume) 30, 31, 49, 74, 111, 116n, 119, 139, 160

'Tower, The' (poem) 92, 108, 110
Townshend, Charles 33, 197
Trilling, Lionel 96
Tsvetaeva, Marina 184, 185, 186, 214
Twelve, The 223–7

Ulysses 90
'Under Ben Bulben' 8

Valéry, Paul 82, 83
Vendler, Helen 7, 28, 29, 60,
    88, 89, 92, 93, 100, 113, 129, 133,
    142, 157, 208, 212
Vico, Gianbattista 50
Villon, François 35
Virgil 35, 146
Vision A, 49, 52, 53, 55, 57, 58, 60,
    62, 74, 78, 79, 82, 83, 85

Wanderings of Oisin, The 104
Weber, Max 33

Wellesley, Dorothy 156
Wesley, Charles 157
Wesley, John 157
Wharton, Edith 46
'Whatever You Say Say
    Nothing' 178
Wheatcroft, Geoffrey 196
Wiene, Robert 33
Wilde, Oscar 58, 204
Williams, Raymond 17
Wimsatt, W. K. 96, 98
Wittgenstein, Ludwig 183,
    211, 212
Wolfson, Susan 102
Wuthering Heights 28

Yeats, George 60, 61, 62,
    63, 67
Yeats, Lily 23

Zizek, Slavoj 16, 220

is generated in both ear and mind'). She recognizes when a metre needs to be 'disturbing' or 'unsettling'. 'A poet ... can silently cooperate with his chosen meter, play ostentatiously with it, or even contend against it'—this goes well beyond mimesis. One of the central stanzas of 'The Statues' 'negates, in every way, the serenity and graciousness of the normative *ottava rima* stanza'.[12] It is an *ottava rima* stanza, but it is crowded with the rhythms and the contents of a graceless world. But in the end Vendler always sees the mess as part of the poem's plan, rather as Attridge finds aptness in unease, and the plan redeems the world's disorder.

I think a partial redemption of this kind must occur in any good poem. If it didn't, the poem wouldn't either satisfy us or worry us, and we wouldn't be able to see what it couldn't redeem. But the great temptation of formalism at its purest (and in some ways at its most splendid) is to make the redemptive act too final and too perfect, and a good deal of the art we care about doesn't redeem disorder at all but narrowly and bravely loses the fight, a version of failure that makes success look small. Everything depends on the margin of the loss, and of course one needs a lot of art, an intense feeling for form, to get any-where near a defeat of this kind. We don't have to be as absolute as R. P. Blackmur, who wrote that 'Thought asks too much and words tell too much; because to ask anything is to ask every-thing, and to say anything is to ask more'. Much thought and many words do nothing of the sort, and there are all kinds of

---

[12] Ibid. 294, 301, 234, 316, 271.

ways of asking less than everything. But Blackmur's hyperbole gestures towards a rare but not hyperbolic truth, and he certainly understands what he calls 'the ultimate failure of imagination itself', which is closely related to what he calls 'the radical defect of thought'.[13]

Of course there is great art that doesn't fail in any sense, and when Yeats said 'the intellect of man is forced to choose | Perfection of the life, or of the work',[14] he didn't secretly mean we are stuck, as Blackmur and Henry Adams thought we were, with the radical imperfection of both. But there is such a thing as the radical imperfection of form, and we shouldn't lose it among form's many undisputed glories. 'It is the triumph of failure', Blackmur says, 'that in the process it snares all that can be snared of what we know'.[15]

This chapter is about what is snared and not snared by form in 'Nineteen Hundred and Nineteen', and the last part of the poem is especially suggestive in this respect, brilliantly failing and succeeding in complicated proportions. Many readers believe that these lines show far more rhetorical swagger than poetic substance, that this otherwise wonderful poem escapes at the end into the sort of historico-spiritualist hocus-pocus Yeats was so fond of. For them Yeats becomes precisely the figure whom 'the reliable citizen', in Seamus Heaney's projection of reason's

---

[13] R. P. Blackmur, *Selected Essays*, ed. Denis Donoghue (New York: Ecco Press, 1985), 224–5, 221.

[14] W. B. Yeats, *The Variorum Edition of the Poems*, ed. Peter Allt and Russell K. Alspach (New York: Macmillan, 1957), 495.

[15] *Selected Essays*, 225.

response to unreason, can see only as a 'charlatan patterning history and predicting the future by a mumbo-jumbo of geometry and Ptolemaic astrology'.[16] I don't disagree with these readers about the swagger or even the hocus-pocus, but the final effect for me is still inordinately powerful, and a sense of failure is part of this power. I want to suggest that the turbulence of the poem, to pick up a Yeatsian word from earlier chapters, its turbulent contents, so to speak, first ironically denied (or ironically recalled as having been denied), then filtered through images of dancing, poetic ambition, and snarling anger, and finally pictured as a shabby but unforgettable apocalypse, are mirrored in the idioms and metres of the work, deflected and tamed by much of its art, but also stalked by a second turbulence, a new strain concentrated almost entirely in the form, the ringing of this poem's uneasy music in our heads, all the troubling residue of the triumph of failure.

II

I should say something about the question of authorial intention. Not that I can settle this long old issue in a quick paragraph or two (or even in a slow book) but every reader makes assumptions in this area and I had better say what mine are.

Generally I think there is much to be said for the now often ignored case against the intentional fallacy, and for the related metaphor of the author's death—that is, for the implication that

---

[16] Seamus Heaney, *Finders Keepers* (New York: Farrar, Straus Giroux, 2002), 106–7.

authors are in an interesting and important sense absent from their texts—that they become their admirers, as Auden said of Yeats, or at least become their readers. A text is defenceless, it just repeats itself, Socrates claimed in the *Phaedrus*, and it can't choose its interpreters ('it has no notion of whom to address and whom to avoid').[17] It also has, or may have, tremendous power, for exactly the same reasons: it just repeats itself, its words don't change even if its meanings do, and interpreters themselves are subject to the rules of whatever language the text uses. This is the source of what Kafka calls the commentators' despair.[18]

Wimsatt and Beardsley were no doubt too extreme in their suggestion that knowledge of an author's intention is 'neither available nor desirable as a standard for judging the success of a work of literary art'.[19] Often unavailable, often interesting, quite often misleading, and always insufficient as a critical measure, would be closer. Borges tells the story of a terrible poem that would be a masterpiece if we referred only to its author's ambitions for it;[20] and if Shakespeare 'did not intend ... anything less than *Hamlet*', as Lionel Trilling once said,[21] it is even truer that he did not write anything less than *Hamlet,* whatever he intended.

[17] Plato, *Phaedrus*, trans. W. C. Helmbold and W. G. Rabinowitz (Indianapolis: Bobbs-Merrill, 1956), 69–70.

[18] Franz Kafka, *The Trial*, trans. Breon Mitchell (New York: Schocken, 1998), 220.

[19] W. K. Wimsatt, Jr., and Monroe C. Beardsley, *The Verbal Icon: Studies in the Meaning of Poetry* (Lexington: University of Kentucky Press, 1954), 3.

[20] Jorge Luis Borges, 'The Aleph', in *Collected Fictions*, trans. Andrew Hurley (New York: Penguin, 1999), 276–8.

[21] Lionel Trilling, *The Liberal Imagination* (New York: New York Review of Books Classics, 2008), 52.

Still, there is something wasteful and disagreeable about not wanting to know what writers think they are doing, and about the accompanying assumption that critics know better. It doesn't seem implausible that writers often achieve what they intend and that their intention has something to do with their achievement. If I find enormous subtleties in a literary work, chances are the writer put them there. The subtle mind at play is the writer's rather than mine. I'm doing what I can but I'm just following clues, not placing them.

A difficulty remains, and significant differences hide within similar critical phrases. A reader's idea of an author's intention is always a guess, if often a good one. This is true even when authors tell us what their intentions are. We don't have to suspect them of lying but neither can we assume they are immune to the ordinary frailties of human self-knowledge. To say nothing of the times when they wish to speak ambiguously, or make a joke.

Long ago a friend and I had a bet about the meaning of a remark made by Philip Larkin, not in a poem but in an interview. In response to a casual mention of Borges, rather like mine a paragraph or so back, Larkin had said, 'Who is Borges?' My friend, the late and much missed Gamini Salgado, took Larkin at his word, thought he was asking a question about a figure whose name he really didn't know. I thought Larkin was pretending ignorance and taking the opportunity to wind the interviewer up a little. I should say that I didn't then and don't now think either of these readings was substantially more plausible than the other. But they were different, Gamini and I each had our preference, and Larkin could hardly have intended both. Finally Gamini wrote to Larkin, consulted the oracle, to borrow the image Wimsatt and Beardsley use for worrying about intention.[22] He received an elegant and courtly reply from Larkin's secretary saying that Mr Larkin was very busy and apologized for not writing himself and hoped it might clear things up for us if he said that in the interview he wished to imply that he rather resented the implication that *everyone* knew who Borges was. Gamini and I were each convinced we had won our bet.

We were guessing and Larkin kept us guessing. When reading a poem we are guessing if we see ourselves as trying to imagine what went on in the poet's mind as he wrote. But if we are just tracking whatever intentionality we find in the words and sentences as we see or hear them, we are not guessing, we are reading, we are exercising our ordinary abilities of comprehension, and the court of appeal is the language itself or more precisely our knowledge of the language and the possibility of trying out our understandings on others who know the language well and care about it.

We can go quite a long way in language without invoking intention at all. Vocabulary and grammar alone will allow me to understand a line like 'Many ingenious lovely things are gone'. I can even hear some of the connotations of the word 'lovely' without thinking of intention since it would be hard for any speaker to take (or want to take) those connotations from it. I begin to need intention—to need to imagine an intention— when I try to hear the overtones, and hear if there are any overtones, in 'ingenious'. Is there a suggestion of small-scale intricate art, wonders of cleverness rather than anything else? If there is,

---

[22] *The Verbal Icon*, 18.

it's picked up a little later in the line 'We too had many pretty toys when young'. But maybe I'm just hearing things, and certainly the mention of Phidias in line 7 suggests I am. His 'famous ivories' were no doubt small but his statues of Athena and Zeus were forty-two feet high.[23] Do I cancel the intention I've imagined or do I keep it and work with it? I don't really want to cancel it and perhaps couldn't, because it sings in the word for me, and the poem seems more interesting with it, even if I now have to deal with apparently conflicting intentions. It's at points like this that readers' choices begin. Different readers choose differently but these are real options, substantive and discussable modes of interpretative action, more like theories or legal opinions than like guesses, and we don't have to imagine the mind of a particular person to get to them. We have only to imagine, as we can scarcely avoid imagining in the presence of any speech act, a tone and a direction for the sentence.

For what it's worth I think Yeats is of mildly uncertain mind about the cultural achievements he lists at the beginning of 'Nineteen Hundred and Nineteen', as if he sees their vanishing written into them, as if the chance of vanishing weakened them even in their prime, and whatever their size. But I can't know Yeats' mind, while I do know that I need to make sense of these shifting connotations and that my experience of the poem is richer for my attempt. Yeats' mind, in other words, is the source of what I am reading and a fascinating subject in its own right, but it can't help me with the poem; and in reality the language of the poem gives me all the help I need, it is the problem and it is the solution, or it is a solution. The language may speak to me differently on another reading, although the words will remain the same.

So when I borrow Blackmur's phrase about the triumph of failure, and speak of a failure that makes success look small, am I saying Yeats intended to fail in this complicated sense? As long as I'm guessing, yes; and I don't mind guessing. But my less speculative claim—I'm not going to call it objective because reading is a personal affair, but I do say it is rooted in the usages and details of a historical language and therefore not merely subjective—is that this is what the words and the order of the words give us to read, and that the words themselves call upon us to do our best by them. Of course they are put together by Yeats and he deserves all the credit for whatever wonder and danger we find in the poem. But the words are not his any more than they are ours, and to be a poet is, among other things, to take one's chances with language.

III

Part I of 'Nineteen Hundred and Nineteen' consists of six stanzas of eight lines, rhymed and metred into a form called *ottava rima*, of which more later. Parts II and III take up what Helen Vendler calls the 'strange stanza' that Yeats invented for 'All Souls' Night'.[24] He also uses it for a section of 'Meditations in Time of Civil War'. This is a ten-line form almost like a truncated sonnet.

---

[24] *Our Secret Discipline*, 69.

Its first six lines rhyme on three sounds in sequence, a-b-c-a-b-c; and its last four lines have an outer rhyme folded about an inner one, d-e-e-d. There are long and short lines, with an interesting arrangement of beats: 5-5-3-5-5-3-3-3-3-5.

Part IV of the poem is a kind of aphorism in four lines, a single stanza of regular tetrameters rhyming in the most (ironically) comfortable way: a-b-a-b. Part V, in a truly amazing bit of invention, uses the same stanza form with an extra line that picks up the second rhyme: a-b-a-b-b. Part VI is a single stanza that returns to the pentameter of the first part of the poem, but with a quite different rhyme scheme. The rhymes go in three-line sequences: a-b-c-a-b-c-d-e-f-d-e-f-g-h-i-g-h-i.

Six parts and five forms, each form bringing with it a different tone and mode, which I'll call—nothing rides on these names except speed of evocation—essayistic (Part I), meditative (Parts II and III) epigrammatic (Part IV), satirical (Part V), apocalyptic (Part VI). If I say that within a single poem Yeats takes us from the world of Addison and Steele to the world of Blake, or even Breughel, crossing something like the terrain of Shelley, La Rochefoucauld, and Swift, you will get a sense of the extraordinary show that is going on. And yet, to pick up the question I already launched, the parts, however different in form and tone, are not separate: the essay continues into the meditation, the meditation lets loose the epigram; the epigram begets the satire; and the satire, in a kind of fortunate fall into violence, is dissolved into vision—or as I shall suggest at the end of this chapter, the next-best thing to vision.

In one of my early fantasies about this book (and about the lectures that were the start of the book), I thought I would devote one chapter or session so solidly to history, so thoroughly soak the argument in material fact, that it would be impossible for anyone to see any conceivable connection to literature or the imagined life at all. The second approach would be exclusively formal, so much a matter of scansion and rhyme and verse form, that it would be impossible to imagine any sort of link to a historical world. Both of these performances were to be impeccable in their exercise of these separable arts, and both were to be supremely boring. The fantasy continued, of course, with rabbits I had not yet found leaping out of hats I had not yet bought, and with a dazzling synthesis of these two apparently irreconcilable perspectives. And that was just a beginning.

Needless to say, I'm not enough of a historian or a formalist to pull either performance off properly, and I didn't find any rabbits, but the polemic in this chapter does belong to the challenge of the fantasy's second section. However, I am not now trying to build a wall; only to pause on one side of a wall that either isn't there or can be got to tumble with only a very little persuasion. As Susan Wolfson says, one of the most damaging restrictions of much formalist criticism has been its desire *not* to give attention 'to the way that formal choices and actions … were enmeshed in networks of social and historical conditions'. But to be enmeshed is not to be swallowed, and Wolfson cogently says that 'poetic forms … demand a special kind of critical attention', an attention that may not be immediately historical in focus but that never ceases, one hopes, to inhabit history. Later she calls this attention 'formalist criticism' rather than 'formalism'.[25] My road

---

[25] *Formal Charges*, 30, 235.

in this chapter leads through highly selected regions of formal analysis. I'm going to talk about some of the uses of rhyme and alliteration in the poem; about the relation of the line divisions of the poem to the grammar of its sentences; and about scansion and metre, often an interesting area of turbulence.

IV

But first I'd like to look briefly at some lexical patterns. Strictly, this is a matter of semantics rather than form, even perhaps a lapse into the New Criticism's bad habit of pretending to talk about form while talking about content all along. But since we can see the repetition of whole words as something like an alliteration of meaning, this glance will, I hope, conveniently set us on the road to more thoroughly formal questions.

The following words, or versions of these words, are repeated within the six parts of the poem: *bronze, image, ivories, grasshoppers, bees, habit, thought, dragon, weasel, work, monument, triumph, break, solitude, vanish, traffic, whirled, wind, shriek, mock, labyrinth.* Some of these terms—*image, thought, work, monument, solitude, labyrinth*—are obviously part of Yeats' general lexicon and frequently or saliently used in his poetry,[26] but if we look at the others we already begin to have a sense of the work the language of this particular poem is doing. It is full of metaphorical or manufactured animals, and the verbs are all busy and troubling and onomatopoeic: *break, vanish, traffic, whirled, shriek, mock.*

---

[26] See Stephen Maxfield Parrish (ed.), *A Concordance to the Poems of W. B. Yeats* (Ithaca and London: Cornell University Press, 1963).

Of course non-repeated words carry a considerable weight in the poem too, and have important echoes elsewhere in Yeats' work: *rule, rage, evil,* for example. *Nightmare,* we may be surprised to find, appears in only two other poems ('The Second Coming' and 'The Gyres'), and *ingenious* and *scot-free* appear nowhere else in the collected verse. But I'll stay for the moment with the repetitions.

Some of them are just that: repetitions. The line in Part I about triumph and solitude returns in Part III with very much the same general meaning as suggested in its first appearance, except that the verb forms have shifted along with the placing in the line: 'would | But break' becomes 'can but mar'. I don't know that there's much to choose between breaking and marring when it comes to solitude, but the thought seems more settled when it returns: not a newly reached conclusion or an ironic 'comfort' but a sort of axiom. It's intriguing that Yeats can make himself seem to arrive at this thought, and then settle for it, since he has been entertaining versions of it since his earliest work. In one of the poems in *The Wanderings of Oisin* (1889) a priest reflects that

> the only good is musing mild,
> And evil still is action's child.
> With action all the world is vexed.[27]

And this is just action, not even triumph.

But a large number of the words that recur in the poem serve not a different purpose—echoes are always supposed to hang

---

[27] *Variorum Edition,* 728.

in our minds—but an intricate additional one. They prolong a first meaning and launch a second. The connotations of a bronze ornament stand at some distance from those of bronzed peacock feathers, and yet the sound and meaning of the word embrace the poem, occurring in the first stanza and the last line. The recurrence is important because it is so firmly placed and marked. Presumably Lady Kyteler's peacock feathers could have been described in almost any number of ways that would have got at their colour. The bronze is there to connect fourteenth-century Kilkenny to ancient Greece, or at least to make us ask what kind of connection there might be. Or is the stronger link or contrast the one between desirous magic and disinterested art? A similar set of questions can be asked about the 'tumult of images' that comes in the wake of Herodias' daughters and the 'ancient image' on the Acropolis, except that the contrast between movement and poise is extreme, and maybe no amount of eager syncretism will really be able to put these cultures together. Perhaps we are to think chiefly of the ephemerality of both? The recurrence of the word 'vanish' also links the first and the last parts of the poem, although the shift of affect is significant. Man may be in love and love what vanishes, but not everything that vanishes can be loved.

Other echoes read more like modulations of an idea, testings of the possibilities of altered contexts. It is one thing, for example, to traffic in artefacts and another to traffic in mockery, but the availability of the idiom makes the two activities seem very close to each other, and we begin to think of crossovers. What else apart from cash do you get from selling objects? Is there an equivalent of a cash value for mockery? Weasels—at least the human weasels the poem is so much concerned with—can shriek with pleasure, but what happens when the wind shrieks? The wind must be doing what it always does: blow. If we hear its sudden force as a form of shrieking, it is because we are ready for a shriek, afraid of being shrieked at.

Winds begin to take over the poem after its stately and sardonic first part. A metaphorical dragon of air, itself a metamorphosis of the dragon that rides our days, falls among the Chinese dancers; there are 'winds that clamour of approaching night'; 'winds of winter', a 'levelling wind', and four mentions of wind in the last part of the poem alone. The winds, it seems, are whatever threatens human activities, but there is a worse threat: what comes after the wind. It is significant that the wind 'drops'—and perhaps has to drop—before the appearance of the frightening last avatars of the poem, the insolent fiend Robert Artisson and his love-lorn admirer. Winds are also associated, in a genuinely riddling way, with a maze. Hard to see what the 'labyrinth of the wind' of the last part would look like or how it would be formed.

The word that recurs most often in the poem—more often than we might imagine and certainly more often than I remembered before I did a careful count—is *thought*. It appears three times in two lines in the first part, but also four times after that, with a range of related meanings. *Thought* as a noun is a piece of moral pretension, 'fine thought', or the thoughts we 'pieced … into philosophy', a form of ambition or mental arrogance closely related to the fantasies lurking in the word 'rule'. Our plan 'to bring the world under a rule' is mocked again in the great later poem 'Meru':

> Civilization is hooped together, brought
> Under a rule, under the semblance of peace
> By manifold illusion;

However, in one of those sharp and tricky turns of which he is a master, Yeats now places thought on the other side of the equation, as a form of human restlessness, the enemy of order.

'Meru' continues

> but man's life is thought,
> And he, despite his terror, cannot cease
> Ravening through century after century,[28]

Thought is both where we hide from our ravening and what makes us go ravening in the first place.

The verb forms of the word are apparently more casual: 'we thought'; 'parliament and king | Thought'; 'nor thought of the levelling wind'. The last usage suggests an absence of all awareness of what is happening, and the first two evoke forms of consciousness well below the level of serious thinking, mere crossings of the mind. The double usage in the single line— 'O what fine thought we had because we thought'—brings together the first meaning I mentioned above and something of the restlessness and complexity of 'Meru'. We had fine thought because we thought. Of course we did, our life is thought, and we have every intention of living fine lives. The surrounding irony and anger of the stanza, of course, collapse this conception completely, suggesting bleakly and crisply that thought itself is

[28] *Variorum Edition*, 563.

error. We get things wrong merely by starting to think, just as we fall into evil, as the priest suggested in the early poem, merely by starting to act. And then the syntax, crossing the verse line, collapses the conception a second time. Not 'we thought' but 'we thought | That ...'—the weakest, vaguest usage of the word possible. We weren't really thinking, just dreaming or assuming, and if we had been thinking we would have been wrong. This interesting complication also eats at the title of the poem in its first published form: 'Thoughts upon the Present State of the World'. Thoughts, it turns out, upon the very idea of thoughts.

Of the non-repeated words *rage* and *evil* especially gain resonance from a comparison of instances in other poems by Yeats. In 'The Lamentation of the Old Pensioner' we learn that 'crazy rascals rage their fill | At human tyranny', although it doesn't seem to do them much good. In 'The Tower' the poet rages against old age—the very rhyme a sort of mockery—and wonders whether others do too. 'Meditations in Time of Civil War' offers us the extraordinary picture of a sort of ghostly soldiery, violent inhabitants of 'the mind's eye', a 'rage-driven, rage-tormented, and rage-hungry troop'. In 'Lapis Lazuli' (and in Shakespeare) 'Lear rages' and in 'Meru' raging goes with ravening and uprooting, ending in 'the desolation of reality'. In 'The Choice', if 'the intellect of man' settles for perfection of the work it is left 'raging in the dark'.[29] When we place these clouds of energetic helplessness around the single use of the word in 'Nineteen Hundred and Nineteen'—

---

[29] *Variorum Edition*, 131, 426, 566, 563, 495.

> That image can bring wildness, bring a rage
> To end all things ...

—we perceive more clearly the noisy pathos of this emotion, its too easy availability and the absence of all alternatives. Rage, perhaps, in these conditions, is itself the expression of an absence of alternatives, and we may glance up the page to find the word 'desolate', anticipating its return as 'desolation' in 'Meru'.

Evil by contrast loses something of the theological force we may want to attribute to the phrase 'evil gathers head', and gains an interesting note of resignation and regret. The arrival or assembly of evil is not a shock or a surprise. It's true that the biblical note is struck in 'The Double Vision of Michael Robartes', where there are apparently prelapsarian 'cold spirits ... knowing not evil and good'. But other uses have a more distending effect. We may think that when the poet reproves the curlew for its complaints, saying 'There is enough evil in the crying of the wind', he is using the term only very vaguely, meaning whatever is distressing or has gone wrong. But when an angry doll screams that

> There's not a man can report
> Evil of this place

—and when we learn that a dying lady has not 'called the pleasures evil | Happier days thought good', we realize the dimensions of the word are often social rather than religious, and if not social, then psychological, as in 'A Prayer for My Daughter':

> to be choked with hate
> May well be of all evil chances chief.

And when in 'The Tower' the poet speaks of a 'worse evil' he means whatever is worse than old age—the death of friends, for example,'or death | Of every brilliant eye | That made a catch in the breath', or various appalling and unnamed because not yet experienced events.[30] The meanings here have deepened since the reproof of the curlew, but not substantially changed, I think. Evil is not wrong but what goes wrong; it is not what we do but what happens to us. This is why its gathering head in 'Nineteen Hundred and Nineteen' is so alarming; and why it is not unconnected with rage, either our own or that of a host of quarrelsome spirits. The extraordinary phrase 'rage-hungry' in 'Meditations in Time of Civil War' catches this note perfectly. Its parallel formations—rage-driven, rage-tormented—make clear the agency of rage: the troop is driven and tormented by it. But is it made hungry by rage, and if so hungry for what? Or is it hungry *for* rage, as anyone may be when the swan has leaped into the desolate heaven?

Rage in 'Nineteen Hundred and Nineteen' gathers strength from Yeats' other uses of the words. *Evil* begins to alter its meaning a little. But the most striking shift comes with the words *rogues* and *rascals*. In the context of this particular poem, where things are about as bad as they can get, the notion that 'the worst rogues and rascals had died out' seems a desperate delusion, something like the belief that crime itself no longer existed. I read the line in this way in my first chapter, and I don't believe such a reading can be entirely wrong. But it can—and does—miss an element of tone, a delicacy in the evocation of the delusion.

---

[30] *Variorum Edition*, 382, 155, 319, 365, 405, 416.

It's only when, prompted by Yeats' other usages or simply by our sense of ordinary language, we think of the exact colouring of the words that we realize what is going on. 'An Hour Before Dawn' opens with 'A cursing rogue with a merry face'; 'The Saint and the Hunchback' gives us 'That great rogue Alcibiades'; in 'High Talk' 'some rogue of the world' has stolen Malachi's stilts. This is not the decline of the west or the end of civilization, and the mitigating effect is extended by the pairing of rogue with rascal. We have seen the crazy rascals raging in 'The Lamentation of the Old Pensioner', but Yeats' most vivid use of this word appears in the splendid poem 'The Three Monuments', also collected in *The Tower*, where Nelson, O'Connell, and Parnell on their separate Dublin pillars are described as 'three rascals' who 'laugh aloud' when politicians talk of purity.[31]

The worst rogues and rascals are not the worst criminals in the world. They are just rogues and rascals, scarcely serious criminals at all. Well, a rogue has perhaps a better claim to be a real offender than a rascal does, and it might be even more fatuous to believe that these characters had died out than to believe in the disappearance of major crime, but that is a different point. In 'Nineteen Hundred and Nineteen' the speaker means to berate his generation for believing in its own high philosophy, but he also suggests, through his tone and vocabulary, that it hides even its lost belief in an act of verbal avoidance. It can name only the milder form of the evils it imagined it had banished, for much the same reason as it calls the supposed achievements of modern civil society mere toys. 'We had many pretty toys when

[31] Ibid., 302, 379, 623, 460.

young' means not 'We regret the civilization we lost' but 'We are now calling toys the elements of the civilization we were idiotic enough to believe we had'.

V

Most of the rhymes in the poem come in pairs, but some come in threes. The return of sounds is an especially delicate effect in *ottava rima*, which is often associated with Italy and Renaissance style, but is also the stanza form of Byron's brilliant and joke-ridden *Don Juan*. Yeats evokes the Renaissance by using the form, hints at rebellion by being very liberal about what counts as a rhyme, and remembers Byron in his angry wit. I'm not quite sure how to read the rhymes of the last stanza of Part I, since with *found* and *found* Yeats offers us what Paul Muldoon calls 'perfect rhyme', i.e. repetition.[32] Going one step further Yeats ends this whole part not only with the same rhyme as in his opening stanza but with the same words: *ivories, bees*. We are back where we started, certainly; but are we surprised to be back or surprised to have made so little headway? What does it mean that words as well as sounds return? Doesn't the very idea of rhyme seem under threat?

In any event, rhyme takes its revenge in Part IV, where the effect is that of a combined surplus and constriction. The rhymes are easy, all regular; the suggestion seems to be that there are plenty more where they come from. This is the world of the

[32] Paul Muldoon, *The End of the Poem* (New York: Farrar Straus and Giroux, 2006), 12.

ballad, almost the jingle. But then when Yeats repeats the same form with an extra line in Part V, the implication is rather different. Now it seems that there are all kinds of words that will keep on making just the same sound, like an angry echo that will not go away; but the echo will return a second time with a light distortion, like a note that having reappeared once as popular music comes back again immediately as sarcasm. Helen Vendler finely says 'the effect is that of climbing up three or four lines and then rapidly losing in a single slide all the ground gained'.[33]

Rhymes and slant-rhymes are distributed fairly equally about the poem—this distribution is one of the reasons this intricate work can seem unusually relaxed about its complex forms. The expectation at the beginning is that the poem is going to be even more relaxed than it is, since it takes six lines to arrive at a full rhyme: stood, wood. Indeed, throughout the poem the full rhymes ring out with special authority, precisely because our ear has been taught not to count on them; and it's tempting to believe they are trying to tell us something, pass on some secret that runs beneath or against the poem's larger argument. Isn't there a story, or the ghost of a story in the appearance of pairs like *chance/prance*, *wrong/gong*, *breath/death*, *rage/page*, *end/mend*, *seemed/dreamed*, *truth/tooth*? I don't want to get carried away here, but the connection of rage to page seems telling, and especially because, as we have seen, the rage is a rage to end all things, and the page is half-imagined, half-written.

The slant-rhymes do seem initially to present an alternative to the rigour of the full rhyme, but gradually they too begin to have

[33] *Our Secret Discipline*, 74.

their recurring, slightly eerie effect, as if a near-miss in sound were also a kind of irony. *Young/wrong, thought/out, cloth/path, air/year*: by the time we get used to hearing these cracked tunes they no longer seem so relaxed, and we can't have missed the careful wrongness of *rule/hole*. That's what it sounds like when philosophers turn out to be weasels. We note too that Yeats uses the word *solitude* three times in the poem, on each occasion fitting it out with an awkward, subdued slant-rhyme: *would, could,* and *good*—a sort of fantasy refrain in its own right. He also uses the word *wind* twice and the word *blow* once, and refuses to provide either of them with anything other than eye-rhymes— *mind, behind, blind,* and *now*. I'm not sure what this says to us, especially since Yeats insisted late in life that he wrote only for the ear. Perhaps there is a pronunciation of these words that will get them close enough to an actual rhyme. But the chance of hesitation still seems important. Given the recurrence of winds in the poem, even in non-rhyming places, the suggestion perhaps is that the whirling weather can't be matched or controlled, can't even be heard, it can only be helplessly seen, watched as it goes about its wrecking work.

   At first glance, alliteration seems to be everywhere in the poem: *many, miracle, multitude, moon* in the first three lines alone. Then *Phidias/famous, golden grasshoppers, too/toys, made/melt, rogues/rascals, teeth/tricks, ploughshare/parliament, days/dragon/ drunken, sleep/soldier, mother/murdered, pieced/planned, signs/ sink, wits/work/whether/wealth, mind/master/mighty/monument, burn/break/bits/bees*. That's just in Part I. After this the intensification of sound lets up a bit, and the second part of the poem has only *right/wrong*—intriguing that these opposites should alliterate, and also look so different on the page—and *goes/gong*. The third part moves back towards the earlier speed—*moralist/ mythological, solitary/soul/swan/satisfied, gleam/gone*—but then calms down again and its last two stanza has only *man/ meditation, lost/labyrinth/laborious/life, winds/winter*,generously spaced out.

Part IV just has *talked/truth* and *shriek/show*, and Part V is in relation to its length even sparser in alliteration. The instances are metrically underplayed too: *late/leave, saw/seasons, good-ness/gay, sick/solitude, mock/mockers*. The last part of the poem seems to be choosing repetition and variation rather than allit-eration, but then the mode comes crowding back towards the end: *dare/daughter/drops/dust, amorous/angry/according/all/are, love-lorn/Lady*, and finally, like a violent stutter or cough, *pea-cocks/combs/cocks*.

Sometimes the device produces only emphasis and isn't asked to do more. This is how *golden grasshoppers, mighty monument, sick of solitude*, and *winds of winter* function. The sound multiplies the sense like a set of aural italics. The interesting cases are the runs of echoes, and at this point we need to think not only of full-blown alliterations (words beginning with the same letter or sound), but all the other resonances within lines and across lines. Internal rhyme or near-rhyme—*seemed/sheer, breast/thrust, dreamed/mend/ seemed/ dreamed*—is the obvious instance, but striking forms of the effect often arise from repeated consonants: the p in *public opinion ripening*, the st, p, and l in *stupid straw-pale locks*, and the astonishing six t's in a row *of trumpeters might burst with trumpeting*.

There are remarkable modulations of consonants in 'Before that brief gleam of its life be gone', where the b's, g's, l's, and f's perform such an intricate dance that the words begin to blur or slither into synonyms, as if *gleam, brief, life,* and *gone* made up a single package. And we might also want to follow out the extraordinary sequencing of the lines I've already quoted more than once:

> Now days are dragon-ridden, the nightmare
> Rides upon sleep: a drunken soldiery
> Can leave the mother, murdered at her door ...

D's give way to r's, *now* is picked up by *nightmare,* which also conceals another r;[34] the l's in *sleep* and *soldiery* and *leave* produce a slackness of sound within these very tight lines, the two s's add to this effect and then the d's return us to drama, the thudding of *-dered at her door* almost silencing what seemed to be the central alliteration of the passage: *mother, murdered.* There's no problem in counting the consonants, and hearing this hard music; but it's very difficult to describe the effect. Essentially it's as if only six letters of the alphabet were doing all the talking here, and as if drunkenness and dragonhood were interchangeable, or at least made of the same moral as well as verbal stuff. If most of the consonants in these lines feel like a direct attack,

---

[34] Yeats wrote six versions of a key phrase here before arriving at the version we know: nightmare/Returning again; nightmare/Can ride again; nightmare/Can ride our sleep; the nightmare/Riding our sleep; the nightmare/Is riding sleep; the nightmare/Riding upon sleep. See *The Tower,* ed Richard J Finneran, with Jared Curtis and Ann Saddlemyer (Ithaca: Cornell University Press, 2007), 200, 218, 232, 234.

a sort of raid, the soft ones complicate the tale: it's easy for bad dreams to escape from sleep into history.

VI

In his essay called 'The End of the Poem', Giorgio Agamben makes a claim 'that, without being trivial, strikes [him] as obvious': 'namely, that poetry lives only in the tension and difference ... between sound and sense, between the semiotic sphere and the semantic sphere'. This is a helpful reminder, and Agamben's next claim takes us even further into the world of form. He suggests that 'the possibility of enjambment constitutes the only criterion for distinguishing poetry from prose'. 'For what is enjambment', he continues, 'if not the opposition of a metrical limit to a syntactical limit?'[35] Enjambment occurs when a poetic line stops, but the sentence or the clause doesn't. Or as John Thompson puts it with elegant and casual clarity, 'In verse the language turns from time to time and forms a new line'.[36] Agamben goes on to say that poems, rather than ending, lapse into prose, since there is no possibility for enjambment with the last line, nowhere else to go: 'the last verse of a poem is not a verse'. A poem finishes, he says, in a sort of state of emergency, since 'sound is about to be ruined in the abyss of sense'. The poem is over, or about to be over; and sound and sense,

[35] Giorgio Agamben, *The End of the Poem*, trans. Daniel Heller-Roazen (Stanford, Calif.: Stanford University Press, 1999), 109.

[36] John Thompson, *The Founding of English Metre* (New York: Columbia University Press, 1961), 4.

perhaps, are 'now forever separated without any possible contact', all tension and even negotiable difference between them gone.[37]

We may be sceptical about the high stakes, all-or-nothing style of this argument, but there is something intriguing about the counter-intuitive claim. We might consider, as we already have, a rival, and more familiar criterion for distinguishing poetry from prose: rhyme. This is certainly not the only criterion—there are plenty of rhymes in prose, although the fact that rhyme is frequent in verse and usually thought to be tasteless in prose might give us some sort of borderline—but rhyme does often seem to finish things, exactly in the way a return to the tonic chord finishes a piece of music written according to a traditional harmonic scheme. That's what the couplets of Shakespearean sonnets always do, what the last two lines of Yeats' *ottava rima* stanza usually do, what the four lines of Yeats' aphorism in 'Nineteen Hundred and Nineteen' brilliantly do: close the story. It is intriguing to think of this apparently all too successful gesture of finality as a secret failure, the poem's pretence at ending what it can only abandon. In such a light, the agent of sound itself, rhyme, the connection of words not by what they mean but by the noise they make, becomes a traitor, gives up the very difference of sense that animated the similarity of sound, and sells itself out emphatically to the world of prose and meaning. 'All this the world well knows', we read, returning to Sonnet 129, 'yet none knows well | To shun the heaven that leads men to this hell'. Well and hell are on the

---

[37] *The End of the Poem*, 112, 113, 114.

same page, so to speak: we well know how far from well we are. This is the end of the poem, rhyme says. Agamben says the poem has died into prose.

James Longenbach is about as far in style from Agamben as one could be, yet, in an elegant new book, he says much the same thing about the poetic line.

Poetry is the sound of language organized in lines. More than metre, more than rhyme, more than images or alliteration or figurative language, line is what distinguishes our experience of poetry as poetry, rather than some other kind of writing.

And again:

The music of a poem—no matter if metered, syllabic or free—depends on what the syntax is doing when the line ends.[38]

Taking this to heart, and looking closely at the relation of line to syntax in 'Nineteen Hundred and Nineteen', we arrive at some interesting notations, and a surprising extension of Longenbach's argument. In Yeats' case there are three actors rather than two: line division, sentence structure according to grammar, sentence length according to punctuation. I'm following the punctuation of the first edition of *The Tower*,[39] where the divisions are lightest—a semi-colon where there is later a colon, a semi-colon where there is later a question mark, a simple absence where there is later an entirely

---

[38] James Longenbach, *The Art of the Poetic Line* (Saint Paul, Minn.: Graywolf Press, 2008), xi, xii.

[39] *The Tower: A Facsimile Edition* (New York: Scribner, 2004).

reasonable comma—but the effect I am describing is present in all editions. The punctuation in all cases tends to stretch the grammar and prolong the sentences. Late in life Yeats said he had sought 'a complete coincidence between period and stanza', but sometimes grammar alone wasn't enough for him.[40]

According to the last of those elements, the way the poem looks as printed, the work has twenty-one sentences, twelve of them making up complete stanzas, that is, stanzas of single sentences. Three stanzas are made up of two sentences, and only one made up of three. The effect of flowing thought is remarkable, and we can get an even stronger feeling for this effect by a simple mechanical device: punctuating according to Yeats' grammar rather than his handwriting or typography. This way twenty-one sentences (by punctuation) turn into thirty-five sentences (by grammar); and only four out of sixteen stanzas are now made up of single sentences. In Yeats' version semi-colons are doing the work of full stops all over the place, and even of a question mark: 'What matter that no cannon had been turned | Into a ploughshare;'. Colons often do the work of full stops too, although with a different and more plausible logic. My purpose here, of course, is not to correct Yeats' practice, or to get him to line up his orthography with his argument—come to that, compared with his spelling, Yeats' punctuation is a model of conventional correctness—but to see more clearly what is happening. The poem, divided into parts, divides those parts themselves as little as possible, pushing syntax into continuity wherever it can

---

[40] *Essays and Introductions* (New York: Collier Books, 1968), 522.

be done, and sometimes when it can scarcely be done at all. This is a poem of several voices, we might say, but it has only one anxiety.

I'm inclined to read this pattern as a variant on Agamben's argument. Yeats is trying to stave off an ending, even of sentences, in a very special sense. It's as if every thought is tracked by another thought, a new qualification or additional sense or instance; as if sentences and poems end not through logical or formal choices but through fatigue—they would go on for ever if they could. This effect is all the more striking, and curiously moving, I think, because such strict logical and formal choices are being made all the time: that's how the shaping of arguments and lines and stanzas works.

And with this effect we get to the poetic line, and what Yeats' grammar is doing when the line ends, or rather certain features of this relation, on which Longenbach says the music of a poem depends. Critics often speak about line-breaks, but Longenbach thinks the term is misleading. The line doesn't break, he says, it just makes way for another line. 'The syntax may or may not break at the point where the line ends.'[41] This description gives us three kinds of relation between line and syntax: the line stops where the syntax does; the line ends where the syntax pauses, at the end of a clause, say, but not at the end of a sentence; and the line ends where the syntax is in mid-flight. For reasons intimately connected with what I have just been saying about the sentences themselves, instances of the first relation are rare in 'Nineteen Hundred and Nineteen'. I count only one according

---

[41] *The Art of the Poetic Line*, 8.

to Yeats' punctuation ('But is there any comfort to be found?');
and get a few more if I follow the grammar ('We too had many
pretty toys when young'; 'I am satisfied with that'; 'The swan
has leaped into the desolate heaven'). All the rest of the line-
endings are of the other sorts: they mark a plausible pause in the
grammar ('Many ingenious lovely things are gone | That seemed
sheer miracle to the multitude'), or they suspend the syntax
itself; the sentence can't go on without our crossing or dropping
down a line: 'The nightmare | Rides upon sleep'; 'for we | Traffic
in mockery', and many more instances.

I want to look at two powerful effects achieved by this last
sort of line. I'm going to call them the follow-on effect and the
rear-view effect. Both moves involve the prolonging of a sentence when it looks as if it could finish, and both use the line
ending to lure us into a false sense of security. The first move
makes you feel that afterthoughts are always preparing some
sort of ambush; the second retroactively alters the meaning of
the sentence. Both of them are versions of what Attridge calls
'meaning in process'.[42]

Here are some examples of the follow-on effect. It functions
rather like those scenes in horror movies where the zombie or
maniac, apparently done with, makes yet another attempt on
our heroine's life. Just when we thought it was safe to assume the
sentence was over, we have to think again.[43] 'A law indifferent to

---

[42] *Poetic Rhythm*, 17.

[43] The effect doesn't have to be troubling. John Thompson points out
that in Turberville's poem 'To an Olde Gentlewoman that Painted hir Face',
the two lines 'that Seemely Rose | Is waxen withered Grasse' could have

blame or praise' was one of the 'many pretty toys' we had when young. But then this same law, in what at first seems merely to be a bit stately rhetorical symmetry, is also said to be indifferent 'to bribe or threat'. This is not at all the same thing; and bribe and threat are on the same (negative) side, not balanced as opposites like praise and blame. This law, if indeed we had it, now seems a sturdier, less ritualized affair, but also, if we had it, always more in danger of being broken or lost. We might even consider, now that we think about it, that praise and blame don't have much to do with the law.

As we have seen, the same 'we' once planned to bring the world under a rule—under a single rule, or under some sort of rule, as distinct from its prior chaos:

> We pieced our thoughts into philosophy,
> And planned to bring the world under a rule ...

Our piecing and our plans have failed, but there is some distance from this failure, however drastic, to what we become when we cross that small space of white paper and read the next line, with its devastatingly casual subordinate clause:

> Who are but weasels fighting in a hole.

We have only to think of Yeats starting a fresh sentence here ('We are but weasels in a hole'), as opposed to a fresh line, to

---

been displayed as a single pentameter: 'That seemely Rose is waxen withered Grasse'. But then we wouldn't have the memory of the lady's beauty that lingers in the pause. 'Without the pause', Thompson says, 'there is in effect only the harsh withered face. With the pause, there are both faces' (*The Founding of English Metre*, 66–7).

see how lethal this effect is, how close these philosophers always were to being weasels—or how they were weasels all along.

And again:

> The swan has leaped into the desolate heaven:
> That image can bring wildness, bring a rage …

This proposition makes good grammatical sense as it is but then we learn that the rage is quite specific, indeed a lot more specific than most rages are:

> a rage
> To end all things, to end
> What my laborious life imagined, even
> The half imagined, the half written page;

The twist of line and syntax points us towards the last part of the poem, and underlines the violence named in the title of this book. A man with a rage to end all things may calm down for a while but he is unlikely to lose his interest in violent endings.

Now some instances of the rear-view effect:

> The night can sweat with terror as before
> We pieced our thoughts into philosophy …

And:

> … habits that made old wrong
> Melt down …

The night can sweat with terror as before—as it used to do all the time, perhaps. No, as it used to do before we started piecing our thoughts into philosophy, an activity now revealed, precisely by the pause and the continuation, as a form of therapy or denial, a pretence of making terror go away. While we were philoso-phizing, we imagined we weren't sweating. This is a strange effect because what should logically and temporally be our first impression becomes our second, and it's important to note that this couldn't happen if we didn't have a practice both of noticing line-endings, feeling tempted to pause at them, and of quickly reading on, because when in doubt we take the logic of the sen-tence rather than the length of the line as a marker of meaning. Here the difference is not as dramatic as the shift from states-men to weasels, and the effect has more to do, I think, with our own slightly shaken interpretative confidence than with any real semantic trouble. We weren't looking for ambiguity and the sen-tence seemed clear enough the first time around. Now we are hesitating, and aren't even sure that our hesitation matters.

With 'Habits that made old wrong | Melt down' we move swiftly into the second line because the logic of the larger sen-tence requires us to. We had 'many pretty toys' when young, and these habits were among them. Melting down old wrong was certainly a fine toy to have, or would have been if we had had it. It would be absurd to think 'habits that made old wrong' could be counted among our cultural and moral achievements even when we are feeling bitter about them. Still, the line does dis-creetly talk back against the logic, the first clause is complete on its own terms. The 'misreading' is all the more tempting because it appears right after the words we have already looked at as part of a follow-on effect, and which were already disturbing the peace of recollection: 'to bribe or threat'. 'Habits that made old wrong', we think, could well be the habits that got us into our

old trouble, that marked the night that used to sweat with terror. No, no, we are talking about habits that got rid of old habits,
these were the habits that made old wrongs melt down, not the
ones that made them. Can't we get this clear, why are we strug-
gling so? Of course we can read the poem without getting into
this trouble, no reason to find Empsonian ambiguities everywhere. But once we have got into this trouble, if we choose to
get into it, the trouble becomes part of the poem, and takes us
deep into its subject: old wrong that failed to melt, habits that
couldn't melt it.

VII

It looks then as if the rhymes and alliterations in the poem largely
reinforce the visible, stated meanings, while the line divisions
often complicate and threaten to unravel whatever argument is
going on. This appearance is far too simple, and I hope to have
hinted in passing that almost every formal effect is subtly different from every other. The differences add up to the variegated
texture of the whole, the shifting tunes and quarrels that make
the work seem both elegant and restless. But the appearance of a
contrast is only too simple, not completely false, and it helps me
to reformulate a truism about the role of form in this poem, and
perhaps in others: that in entertaining its various relations with
whatever is not form—relations of counterpoint, confirmation,
complication, contradiction, expansion and so on—form shifts
the location of the poem from the page (or the place where the
poet's voice is literally sounding) to the pulses and minds of
the readers, turns it into something that is already happening

whether we know it or not, a drama of which whatever overt meaning we take away is only a part. This suggestion is obvious enough, I know—obvious, but not trivial, I hope, to borrow Agamben's terms—but I need to insist on it in order to make the next move in this chapter: the turn to metre and scansion, where I believe this performance finds its fullest incarnation. In an essay on metre, W. D. Snodgrass writes of sharing a 'complex of connections'.[44]

The poem opens and closes in iambic pentameter, perhaps the most familiar form of line in English poetry, although the rhythms are more varied in Part VI. The metres of Parts II and III are intricate and relaxed and only some fairly inventive scansion can produce continuing regularity in these stanzas. Parts IV and V return to a sharp regularity, making clear that we are in the worlds of epigram and satire.

Auden said Pound made the spondee 'respectable in English verse';[45] but Yeats makes it rife. Paul Muldoon writes of the 'predominantly spondaic' lines in 'All Souls' Night',[46] and there are spondees, or what may be read as spondees, all over 'Nineteen Hundred and Nineteen': *fine thought, worst rogues, now days, nightmare, scot-free, brief gleam, all break, all turn, wind drops.* The thumping effect is very strong, often set off by a marked lightness elsewhere in the line. Think for instance of 'Wind shrieked—and where are they?' We could stress 'wind'

---

[44] W. D. Snodgrass, 'The Use of Meter', *The Southern Review* (1999), 806.

[45] Quoted in Edward Mendelson, 'Introduction', *W H Auden: Prose, Volume III (1949–1955)* (Princeton: Princeton University Press, 2007), xx.

[46] *The End of the Poem*, 8, 13.

or 'shrieked' or both; and surely both is going to be a favourite option.

Thompson writes of the 'tension between the reality of experience represented by the intonations of speech and the form of artifice',[47] and Derek Attridge speaks of a similar tension, although he might want to gloss this fine description by saying the tension is between two modes of reality, or two experiences, rather than between reality and form. Milton, according to Robert Bridges, '*scanned* his verse one way and *read i*t another'.[48] Yeats certainly offers us many wonderful instances of divergence or hesitation between metre and anything like idiomatic pronunciation. Angela Leighton reminds us of Robert Frost's account of these matters. 'Poetry plays the rhythms of dramatic speech on the grid of metre.' And again: 'Footbeats for the metre and heartbeats for the rhythm'.[49] Yeats himself wrote of reading the opening line of *Paradise Lost* in two or even three different ways, counting the feet in one mode and crossing the verse with 'passionate prose' in another.[50] Angela Leighton, thinking specifically about Yeats, offers a memorable variation on these formulas: 'Metre never misses a beat, but rhythm can let you hear the heart stop.' 'Yeats', she adds, 'is a master of such contrary speeds.'[51]

I want to concentrate on some rather difficult and lurid examples of such speeds, but shall mention one simpler, although very

---

[47] *The Founding of English Metre*, 127.
[48] Ibid. 5.
[49] *On Form*, 152, 151.
[50] *Essays and Introductions*, 524.
[51] *On Form*, 153.

elegant case, where the scansion gives us one kind of idiomatic, although perhaps not immediately obvious reading; and a 'natural' pattern of emphasis gives us something else. We could read the following line in this way:

> Mán is in lóve and lóves what vánishés ...

The last stress is very faint but our ear has become accustomed to five beats and easily supplies it. But what about taking the line as an absolutely regular iambic one? Then we get

> Man ís in lóve and lóves what vánishés ...

A little more strident, more anxious, less stately—although we get this effect by following a convention almost too literally.

Metrical difficulty arises in 'Nineteen Hundred and Nineteen' when the stanza form itself becomes uncomfortable, as Helen Vendler says of the second and third parts of the poem. The capaciousness of the same stanza in 'All Soul's Night' arises chiefly from the easy alternation of regular rhythm and changing line-length; and when the rhythm breaks from regularity, it breaks into extra emphasis rather than getting lost. This is how the spondees work, and how the opening lines, in particular, acquire what Paul Muldoon calls their 'extraordinary combination of the incantatory and the carefree'.[52] But this is not at all the feeling the stanza creates in 'Nineteen Hundred and Nineteen'. So many lines here sound like prose that we wonder not only how to scan them but whether they should be scanned at all: 'Some moralist or mythological poet'; 'I am satisfied with

---

[52] *The End of the Poem*, 9.

that'. It's only when we read the rhyme on 'poet', and reach the repetition of 'satisfied' that we realize that formal or musical demands are being made of us, and we wonder what they are. But the effect begins earlier, with the opening line of Part II. No spondees here, and no rhythm at all that's easy to settle on:

> When Loie Fuller's Chinese dancers enwound ...

There are all kinds of interesting snags in the line. *Loie* sounds as if it might be a monosyllable, so we are not quite sure where to go with it. *Chinese* seems to require the pronunciation *Chínese* if the line is to get launched. And *wound* is a little perturbing, with its uncertain phonetics, double meaning, and odd prefix. Still, we can get to a scansion if we have to:

> When Lóie Fúller's Chínese dáncers enwóund ...

Four iambs and an anapaest; or in Derek Attridge's terminology, a five-beat line with an extra off-beat towards the end. It does feel as if we are working too hard, though, and it may be worth imagining what this line's regular if imaginary cousin might look like:

> When Láura Fúller's éager dáncers wóve ...

It's clear that Yeats wanted his awkwardness, and indeed it runs through the whole of the two parts using this stanza. A beat does get established in this second part, and indeed the rhythm of the second line repeats that of the first exactly, if more gracefully, establishing a pattern ('A shíning wéb, a flóating ríbbon of áir'), and the third line, with its two anapaests ('It séemed that a drágon of áir) positively skips. And then all is well until the last line but one of this part:

All men are dancers and their tread …

It scans readily enough into four beats (All mén are dáncers
ánd their tréad), even if the stress on *and* is a little sing-songy;
but the insertion of a fourth beat where the stanza-form, here
and in the other poems where Yeats uses it, requires only
three, is more than a little strange, and it's strange too that it's
so difficult to get this line to go into a three-beat framework.
Reading *Áll men* rather than *All mén* doesn't solve any problems. The trick is to prevent any of the three successive offbeats
('dáncers and their tréad') from turning into a beat. What we
do (what I do), is refuse the four-beat line out of loyalty to the
felt rhythms of the poem so far, but fail to settle the three-beat
question. The feeling of the line is undoubtedly connected to
the blunt word 'tread', induced by its rhyme-partner 'instead'
but still a rather flat-footed term for dancers; and the combination of suspended rhythm and asserted argument here is
distinctly upsetting. It creates only a little hope or diversion by
allowing the thought that if these men and women are dancing
to a harsh repetitive destiny they are not doing it very well, and
perhaps they are not dancing at all, just plodding, prisoners
rather than performers.

Part III opens with similar rhythmical hesitations, as we have
seen, and similarly runs into the threat of a four-beat line at 'Í
am sátisfíed with thát'. We can stave off the threat by scanning
'I am sátisfíed with thát', but racing through 'I am' is awkward,
and 'satisfied', like 'solitary' or 'moralist' or 'mythological' or
(later) 'labyrinth', makes a limp and sprawling sound, seems
either too obliging metrically or just not at home in song at

all—unless we go for that tempting four-beat line, and then the thing seems mechanical. Yeats is asking us, I think, or asking our pulse or our ear, to register what it feels like to be on the edge of verse, not quite in and not quite out of the order of the poem. Then he lets us off the hook, and the rhythm settles down. 'Whether to play or to ride' half-imitates the rhythm of 'It seemed that a dragon of air'; lightness and the chance of action enter the work again. There's a brief hitch while we wonder what to do with 'Is lost amid the labyrinth that he has made'. The word 'that' shifts the stress from 'he', and the line itself, starting so firmly and ending in a mundane hurry, mimics the man's condition. But then the stanza form settles into fast, hard, self-accusing music:

> O but we dreamed to mend
> Whatever mischief seemed
> To afflict mankind, but now
> That winds of winter blow ...

And the wonderful last line, unlike all the others in these two parts of the poem, offers neither regular beats nor a diffusion of stress but a startling richness of metrical options, each producing a slightly different meaning. The underlying rhythm, set up convincingly by the previous lines, is a basic iambic beat: 'Learn thát we wére crack-páted whén we dréamed'. But it's also possible to stress 'Learn', 'we' and 'crack'. The line presents us with a kind of ironic wealth: so many ways of saying what we got wrong, so many places to lay the blame—as if the difference between 'we wére' and 'wé were', for example, represented quite distinctive arraignments.